"In this accessible volume, A.V. Flo[...]
cally interweaves personal experie[...]
understanding of how the nervous system adaptively shifts bodily states to support survival in the short term, while simultaneously disrupting the essence of being human, our health, and our ability to connect, co-regulate with loved ones, and compassionately witness another's trauma. As our societal institutions become more trauma-informed, *Disrupting the Bystander* documents the impact of abuse and violation of trust on our ability to create relationships, maintain health, boldly and curiously explore opportunities, and maintain a purposeful life."

—Stephen W. Porges, PhD, Distinguished University Scientist and Founding Director of the Traumatic Stress Research Consortium in the Kinsey Institute, Indiana University and professor of psychiatry at the University of North Carolina

"*Disrupting the Bystander* combines deep theory and intensely practical advice, creating an essential handbook for supporting those who have been harmed, while also caring for yourself. If you've ever felt helpless in the face of someone else's discomfort or pain, this book will teach you how to show up and stand up."

—Laszlo Bock, CEO of Humu and author of *Work Rules! Insights from Inside Google to Transform How You Live and Lead*

"The emotional wisdom and depth of research in this book is incredible. Anyone supporting someone through trauma needs this book."

—Aleatha Parker-Wood, machine learning and privacy researcher

"This is a valuable and unique book, combining deep sensitivity and empathy with a rigorous, evidence-based approach to the best ways to handle some incredibly difficult situations. A.V. Flox faces hard questions with bravery, honesty, and relentless practicality. Her answers contain something valuable for all of us."

—Sean Carroll, author of *Something Deeply Hidden*

"I'm both thrilled and relieved that A.V. Flox's important work is now unleashed upon the world. Our communities need better guidelines for reducing harm, ones that are informed by neuroscience and the mechanics of trauma, and I can't think of a more meticulous and conscientious author to handle the task."

—Arden Leigh, creator of The Re-Patterning Project and frontwoman of Arden and the Wolves

"A must-read for anyone interested in repairing harm in their communities. Using a combination of personal narrative and research, Flox provides a map for helping others to heal while continuing to hold abusive individuals accountable. Reading this book helped me learn more about my responses to my own trauma, as well as to the trauma of others. With this map in place, I know that I will move forward as a better friend, activist, survivor, and person. We all know people who have been harmed and people who have harmed. This is why everyone should read this book."

—Kelly Sundberg, author of *Goodbye, Sweet Girl: A Story of Domestic Violence and Survival*

Disrupting the Bystander

Disrupting the Bystander

When #metoo Happens Among Friends

A.V. Flox, with a foreword by Feminista Jones

Disrupting the Bystander
When #metoo Happens Among Friends
Copyright © 2019 by A.V. Flox

Thorntree Press, LLC
P.O. Box 301231
Portland, OR 97294
press@thorntreepress.com

Thorntree Press's editorial offices are located on the ancestral, traditional and unceded lands of the Musqueam, Squamish and Tsleil-Waututh nations.

Cover design by Lara Minja/Lime Design
Interior design by Jeff Werner
Substantive editing by Andrea Zanin
Copy-editing by Heather van der Hoop
Proofreading by Hazel Boydell and Sandra Ann Miller
Indexing by Catherine Plear
Sensitivity critique by Angel Adeyoha, Bianca Laureano, M'kali-Hashiki and
      Noemi Martinez
Library of Congress Cataloging-in-Publication Data
Names: Flox, A. V., author.
Title: Disrupting the bystander : when #metoo happens among friends /
      A.V. Flox.
Description: Portland, OR : Thorntree Press, [2019] |
Identifiers: LCCN 2018009774 (print) | LCCN 2018013153 (ebook) |
      ISBN 9781944934576 (epub) | ISBN 9781944934583 (mobipocket) |
      ISBN 9781944934590 (pdf) | ISBN 9781944934569 (softcover : alk. paper)
Subjects: LCSH: Bystander effect. | Helping behavior.
Classification: LCC BF637.H4 (ebook) | LCC BF637.H4 F57 2019 (print) |
      DDC 302.34--dc23
LC record available at https://lccn.loc.gov/2018009774

10 9 8 7 6 5 4 3 2 1

Printed in the United States of America.

To Mary, whom I promised.

"Our common human experience is to feel soothed in the presence of others and distressed when we are left behind."

— *Deb Dana*

"Humans have a biological imperative to connect."

— *Stephen W. Porges*

Contents

Acknowledgments

I am in the debt of all those who've ever called on me to address the harms I have done. I hope to honor their courage and love by continuing to do the work to change. I'm also grateful for those who have pulled me aside to let me know when friends of mine were causing harm, as well as those who have shared access to whisper networks as a means of harm reduction. These actions may seem small, but they are immense. They are how we change the world. I extend gratitude and solidarity to the survivors who have trusted me with their experiences and allowed me to hold space for them. Their courage is contagious.

I am indebted to Mimi Kim, whose work through Creative Interventions changed my life, as well as Betty Martin, who showed me how I could use my own hands to return to my body and build my somatic sense of safety. I extend my gratitude as well to INCITE!, Mariame Kaba, Bianca Laureano, Aida Manduley, Nora Samaran, Mia Mingus, Tada Hozumi, Jessica Lanyadoo, Shaunga Tagore, Michelle Lisa Anderson, Audacia Ray, Tara Burns, Kate D'Adamo, Melissa Gira Grant, Jini Patel Thompson, Güliz Ünlü, Stephen W. Porges, Tage Rai, and so many others whose work has informed my worldview.

I owe a debt to all those who welcomed me into their communities, showed me new ways to look at things, modeled courage in confronting harm, and offered me encouragement along the way: Alex Morgan, Angel Adeyoha, Arikia Millikan, Ava James, Azura Amethyst, Bethany Brookshire, Calum Campbell, Cara Santa Maria, Carin Bondar, Carmen Leilani De Jesus, Catherine Plato, Charlie Starr, Chelsey

Blair, Christina Marie, Cleo Dubois, Damien Basile, Danielle Roberts, Daphne Mir, Darshana Jayemanne, Deborah Blum, Denise Tanton, Dolores Tejada, Ed Yong, Elisa Camahort Page, Elisa Vegas, Ella Mové, Emily Finke, Erin Kennedy, Eva Blake, Eva Gantz, Eve Minax, Eve Rickert, Feminista Jones, Gretchen McGhie, jackie summers, Jacqueline Steiger, Jacquelyn Gill, Jakob Liljenwall, Jade Desires, Janet Stemwedel, Jen Hazel, Jennifer Ouilette, Jessamy Barker, Joanne Manaster, Jolie O'Dell, Jonathan Eisen, Jory Des Jardins, Julie Vanderlee, Justin DeKom, Julie Ross Godar, Kara Kimbria, Kate Clancy, Katherine Mancusso, Katherine Gerardi, Katy Chalmers, Kelly Shibari, Kelly Sundberg, Kenzi Connor, Kitty Stryker, Lea Kissner, Leslie Pollock, Lily Garcia, Lisa Stone, Liz Neely, Louisa Leontiades, Luciano Garbati, Maryn McKenna, Matthias Schwenteck, maymay, Megan O'Brien, Michael Takatsuno, Mihal Davis, Mineh Dee, Monica Kovacs, Moxxy Cox, Ning Cai, Petra Hunter, Race Bannon, Raychelle Burks, Robyn Dalzen, Rose Eveleth, Rugger Ducky, Sam Manewitz, Sarah Lester, Scout Tran, Sean Carroll, Shira Lipkin, Stephanie Brooker, Susan Mernit, Susan Schuster, Tara Farrell, Tas Al-Ghul, Tom Leidy, Trudes Tango, and Zane Rose.

In particular, I wish to thank Angel Adeyoha, M'kali-Hashiki, Noemi Martinez, Bianca Laureano, and Andrea Zanin for their feedback on the manuscript, as well as Sandra Ann Miller, Heather van der Hoop, and Hazel Boydell for their edits. Special thanks to Bailee DesRocher at Beautiful Critters for bringing my orca pod to life, Lara Minja for the colorful cover, and Jeff Werner for the gorgeous formatting. I offer my gratitude also to the Bay Area Transformative

Justice Collective, which allowed me to use their Pod-Mapping Worksheet, as well as Stanley Rosenberg, for permission to include his Basic Exercise.

More than anything else, I am grateful for the people in my life, especially my accomplice and lover in arms, Yonatan Zunger, and my dear friends Cassandra Hamman, Dean Skibinski, Aleatha Parker-Wood, Aaron Wood, Anne Hodder-Shipp, Jason Goldman, Buddhini Samarasinghe, Melissa Jun Rowley, Laurie Percival, Arden Leigh, and Virgil, who showed up for me in innumerable ways during this descent.

Foreword

Author's note*: The following account is as important as it is powerful. However, as with any survivor testimony, its contents may be activating for any reader and triggering for other survivors. Please check in with yourself—before and as you read—and listen to your body. Remember that you are in control here: you can read on, or you can pause and circle back after taking care of yourself.*

Content note*: Brief descriptions of various harms, some involving children.*

—A.V.F

§

The first time I became aware of my body as a sexual object, I was four years old. I was taking a nap at my childcare provider's house when her eleven-year-old son lay on top of me and began pressing his body against mine, making what we call "dry humping" movements. At that age, I had no idea what was happening, but I distinctly recall him saying "Shhh" in my ear. He did this several times over several days, his hands sometimes roaming over my small body, and I never said a word. My young mind could not process what was happening and, for several years, I blocked it out. The vivid memories would come back to me later in life during one of the several sexual assaults I experienced as an adult.

The first time I became aware of my body as a desirable object, I was eleven years old. I was walking home from school and a much older man was walking behind me, making lewd comments and trying to get my attention. Though I was nearly six feet tall at that young age, it was very clear from my young face, book bag, and school clothing that I was a child. I remember feeling terrified, not knowing if he was just saying those words because he was a nasty old man or if he planned on acting on his desires for me, a child. I sped up and prayed that I would make it home safely. Again, I never said a word about what happened.

In fact, I have not spoken a word about most of the incidents of sexual harassment and assault that I have experienced in my forty years of life. I speak vaguely of them, making points to identify myself as a survivor and to connect with others who may feel less alone or even empowered by my admissions. I rarely go into detail about the things that have happened because a part of me still feels like I won't be believed, that despite being a prominent advocate for victims of sexual assault, I will be shamed or ridiculed, and that maybe some of it was my fault.

It's difficult to come forward when you have been victimized, especially repeatedly, because you're often left wondering, "How did this happen to me?" I'm educated, successful, intelligent, beautiful, and strong, so how can *I* be anyone's victim? How could *I* have allowed these things to happen to me? Where is my power? The process of reconciling these conflicts is a long, difficult one that requires not only internal reflection but also help from others. The more I have been reminded that this journey cannot be made alone, the stronger I have felt. My decision to not only be more open about my own experiences, but also to help others who have struggled with similar things, has led to my work as an activist in this space.

In the summer of 2014, I shared a story on Twitter about witnessing street harassment in New York City. As I was prone to do, I shared what had happened immediately after it took place. A young mother was pushing a stroller when a man approached her, trying to engage her in a conversation she clearly did not want to be part of. She declined his advances several times, but he kept going, following her down the street, at one point even reaching out to grab her. I was with my son, and as I watched this situation, I could not help but intervene. I went over to the woman and asked her, while not acknowledging the man, "You OK, sis?"

What ensued was a battle with an ego borne of toxic masculinity—his feeling of entitlement to her attention and the perceived threat of a bystander's intervention led him to react angrily and focus his anger toward me. While he and I argued, the woman and her child got away safely, which was the outcome I sought. He could not abide me interrupting him, as he said he was just trying to make money to feed his daughter. Well, to me, it seemed like he was harassing a woman who did not want his attention, but I indulged him. After all, who can't respect a good hustle? (He was selling CDs on the street in 2014, but who am I to judge?) What I witnessed was more about him feeling disrespected by me and less about him feeling his business was being infringed upon. He felt that by asking if the woman was OK, I was suggesting that he was problematic or a threat, and that did not jibe well with him.

The man was a threat, though he did not see himself as one. He believed he had the right to approach anyone on the street, talk to them even after they had declined, grab their bodies, and follow them as they tried to get away. For all intents and purposes, that behavior is quite threatening, but he did not see it as such. And he is not alone, as I have come to better understand.

From this experience, and subsequent conversations about it on Twitter, came the creation of the "You OK, Sis?" campaign, or #YouOKSis. The idea I shared was that we should all become more vigilant when it comes to street harassment, and I issued a call to action that summer, asking people to interrupt street harassment to ask victims if they were "OK." Because I focused on the victim, not the harasser, I centered her needs in the moment, which has not been the traditional approach. Too often, the inclination is to go after the harasser and try to get them to back off, but that approach risks an escalation that can lead to more violence. The harasser could feel offended by my intervention and react violently to prove himself as a man, a response many boys are taught to have when someone else encroaches on what they believe is theirs. Boys and men are also socialized to prove their manhood through protection, jumping in to help a damsel in distress by challenging her (likely male) threat and saving the day. Too often, this approach leads to fights, injuries, or, in rare cases, death.

While in the instance that inspired #YouOKSis, the man reacted negatively and I got into a verbal spat with him, generally, focusing on the person being harassed is an effective intervention to defuse these situations. I began to use #YouOKSis as a way to encourage conversation not only about bystander intervention tactics that could better defuse street harassment and support victims, but also about the unique street harassment experienced by women of color, Black women in particular.

This was not the first time I spoke publicly about street harassment—I had been writing about it for several years on my blog, as well as having open conversations about it. But, this was the first time I felt like something more needed to be done to specifically amplify the voices of Black and Latina women, who had been all but erased from mainstream discussions about street harassment, but who are in fact more likely to experience it and more likely to experience physical violence and death as a result of it. Movements like Holly Kearl's Stop Street Harassment and Emily May's Hollaback! have worked hard to study the extent to which street harassment affects women, and how laws do or do not protect victims. Their data has been invaluable in supporting efforts to end street harassment and support those who have suffered alone and in silence. However, these movements have primarily featured White women as the faces of victims and men of color as the perpetrators, which is not a realistic representation.

The truth is, Black and Latina women experience street harassment more intensely, frequently, and fatally for various reasons. First, we are more likely to live in environments where foot traffic is heavy and we rely more on public transportation where we live and work. Harassment happens mostly as women walk down the street and are exposed to harassers who linger there, so women in urban areas are more likely to be subjected to it. While street harassment affects women of all races, when we consider the disproportionate number of Black and Latina women living in urban areas, the rates go up.

Second, women of color are more likely to live and work in lower-income neighborhoods. Where there is high unemployment among men, there is a higher incidence of street harassment, as the unemployed men spend more time "hanging out" on the street, looking for something to do. For some of these men, the simple act of yelling something obscene at a woman reinforces their manhood; getting a reaction, whether positive or negative, makes them feel seen, heard, and acknowledged. For economically disenfranchised men, these types of quick power grabs have lingering harmful effects on women.

Third, women of color are hypersexualized at a young age, so we begin experiencing street harassment as early as ages 10 to 12. A significant body of research suggests Black children are seen as older, and Black girls, especially, are pegged as "fast" or hypersexual even before experiencing puberty, so we are often treated as sexual objects before we are seen as people.[1] When #YouOkSis began, I had been experiencing street harassment almost daily for twenty-four years. More than two decades of dealing with the harassment had taken its toll on me, and I believe that motivated me to act as I did that day. I had finally had enough of the suffering in silence and could not bear to see another woman endure what I had experienced, likely for longer than she had been alive.

Finally, harassers whose victims are Black and Latina face fewer consequences, and they know it. Racism in America has created a hierarchy of value among people, and when it comes to women, White women are at the top of the list. When White women are victims of harassment, perpetrators face stiffer consequences and harsher sentences than they do when women of color are their victims—that is, if any consequences are actually enacted at all. As a result, when street harassment or rejection of a man has led to a woman's death, the overwhelming majority of the victims have been Black and Latina women. From Mary Spears in Detroit, killed when she refused to give her phone number to a man after attending a funeral, to Islan Nettles, killed because her harasser was teased for being attracted to a trans woman, Black women have been the primary victims of aggressive, fatal street harassment. Centering our stories and creating a supportive community has long been the

....

1   P.R Lockhart, "A New Report Shows How Racism and Bias Deny Black Girls Their Childhoods," Vox, May 16, 2019, https://www.vox.com/identities/2019/5/16/18624683/ black-girls-racism-bias-adultification-discipline-georgetown

primary goal of #YouOKSis, and over the last few years, support for the movement has only grown.

It has become increasingly important to have more conversations about what we experience because remaining silent about harm only signals acceptance. As writer Zora Neale Hurston once said, "If you're silent about your pain, they'll kill you and say you enjoyed it." Speaking truth to power has been a vital tool in the war against these acts of violence. And we must call it what it is: violence. Whether verbal, emotional, or physical, harassment of all forms, from all people, in all spaces is violence. We can no longer hide in shame and allow ourselves to accept blame and internalize what was done to us.

Disrupting the Bystander is a call to action for those who seek not only solidarity and healing, but valuable tools to move forward and be part of "the work." In it, you will find valuable resources, tangible actions, and appropriate language for creating conversations, challenging the status quo, and speaking your truth into your power. It is a powerful guide to engaging survivors with delicacy, working toward empowerment beyond victimhood, and challenging ourselves to think beyond what we believe we already know, so we can be better. There is no one perfect solution for helping people who are being victimized or who have survived trauma, but there are best practices, and you will find them in these pages.

I encourage you to read with an open mind to learn how you can better empathize, find tools to help you heal, and take to heart the invaluable guidance in this book. We are all in this together, and if we find our focus, hone in on our passion, and commit to doing the work and moving forward, we will bring about the change needed to make this world safer for generations to come.

Feminista Jones, author of *Reclaiming Our Space: How Black Feminists Are Changing the World from the Tweets to the Streets.*

Introduction

We were not prepared for #metoo when it blew up on Twitter in October 2017.[2] In many ways, we still aren't. What do we do when we learn a friend has been harmed? And what does it mean to be a good friend when someone we love is the one who caused the harm?

We live in a society that confines survivors to silence and where our only avenues for addressing harm do little to prevent its recurrence. Trapped within a binary of silence or punishment, it's no wonder so many of us remain paralyzed even as the disclosures continue to come. Punishment requires both certainty and authority, which most bystanders lack. But the silence has been broken, so we cannot comfortably return to it. Few of us are strangers to the nagging feeling within that paralysis. We intuit—correctly—that we have some kind of responsibility when harm occurs in our communities and circles of friends, but what is it? And if we have responsibility, do we have rights?

§

Ten years ago, a friend and I met up for drinks, and without warning, she told me that she'd been harmed by someone in our circle of friends. The disclosure came out of left field, and I wanted to be helpful, but I didn't know how. The only two options I knew were silence and punishment.

....

2   The Me Too movement was founded in 2006 by Tarana Burke. When I say it blew up on Twitter, I mean that it went viral, not that it began.

I'd been brought up to aspire to silence as a rule. This silence was not the kind that accompanies peaceful moments. It was the silence of distance—the gap where the truth should be. To share negative situations like health problems, financial troubles, or experiences of harm was to upset and disturb, and in my family, that just wasn't done—not until the trouble had passed and the experience had been properly editorialized into something uplifting, charming, or, at the very least, appropriately inoffensive. As long as a misfortune remained active, regardless of gender, we were expected to face it with the effortless grace of marble statuary.

Though I rebelled, as black sheep and teenagers do, I did nevertheless internalize the toxic beliefs that enable so many family members I love and respect to act as foot soldiers in the army of collusion. I may not be *comfortable* with silence, but I can still long for it—captivity can look a lot like peace if you're willing to overlook a few critical details.

Of course, once the silence is broken—as it was on the evening my friend told me what she had been through—it ceases to be an option, leaving only punishment.

It was punishment I was thinking about when she spoke again, uttering the words that would lead me out of the binary once and for all: she asked me to write. Maybe not about what had happened to her specifically—she wasn't sure she wanted to invite people to scrutinize her experience—but about sexual assault, how agency can be undermined, how friends can fail to intervene. As we rattled off ideas, the desolation and futility that had settled in my heart disappeared. In their place appeared something resembling hope: the ache of knowing she'd been hurt remained, but I could *do something*. I could do something that had meaning for her—and it happened to be something I had the skill to do.

I have thought about this moment many times over the years and the way it influenced the trajectory of my work as a journalist. Sex was my beat then, so writing about certain kinds of harms wouldn't have been a large departure. But at the same time, sex was something of a Trojan horse[3] for me. Early on, I'd realized people would read anything if they thought they were reading about sex: math, quantum mechanics, chemistry, genomics, botany, paleontology—even intellectual property law. This worked out great for me in a saturated media landscape where women were not often assigned very technical pieces. But it also meant that such a messy, human, and profoundly visceral topic like harm felt more than a bit foreign to me.

We all start somewhere.

§

In the autumn of 2013, one, and then two, and then three women came forward to name the harm they had experienced at the hands of a man I knew.

When the silence about a harm is broken, for as long as we remain in the binary, the only other option is punishment. As a result, the impulse to *do something* among those who loved this man became twisted. Instead of helping him understand what had led him to develop this pattern

----

3   During the siege of Troy, the Greek army built a huge wooden horse and used it to smuggle their troops within the city walls.

of harm, and what measures we could take to prevent it from recurring as he undertook the work to change, many of us began to speak highly about his contributions. Some of those who loved him even attacked the women who had come forward.

In 2013, I didn't know how to help someone become accountable for their harm. When I messaged with him, I had only the wherewithal to tell him to call off those who were defending him and attacking survivors. I reminded him that it takes immense courage for people who experience harm to come forward and name someone in a position of power. He listened to me, and he did what I requested. Today, I ask myself whether, had I known then what I know now, he would have worked with me and others through a full accountability process. Unfortunately, I didn't know about that option at the time. The only people who provided him with next steps were his employer's attorneys—and their primary goal was to minimize liability for his employer, not guide him to accountability. They recommended silence, and he listened. Our professional community, unsure about how to safeguard itself from additional instances of harm at his hands, expelled him.

As the years passed, my friend hardened and forgot the impact of his harm. He came to believe that he had been wronged by a hysterical mob on the internet, and we drifted apart as a result. I agree that he was wronged, but not by a hysterical mob. It was us—his friends—who did wrong, hurting not only him, but those he harmed, as well as our entire community. We missed the opportunity to help him fully own his harm, begin the work to change, and make reparations to those he harmed and to the community at large for the trust he had broken.

This failure followed me, as failures tend to, like a gosling that had imprinted on my boot. When another friend came to me three years later to tell me that he, too, had done harm, the gosling was still there waddling behind me. But what could I do? I was just a journalist.

"I wish I had the skill set to do something about this that is constructive," I told my friend. I would hatch a second gosling before I realized that there was nothing preventing me from developing that skill set. After all, if there's one thing a journalist is supposed to be good at, it's asking questions. I had many questions.

Eventually, I would go on sabbatical from freelancing to focus exclusively on how best to support people who had been harmed and people who were harming. And it wouldn't be a moment too soon, as it turned out—within a year, #metoo would hit Twitter, catalyzing a wave of disclosures and callouts in many more of my communities.

I could write a whole other book about the places I've been and teachers I've learned from on this journey. As a journalist, my initial inclination was to search for authority figures—the people we look to when harm occurs, such as those who work in the criminal justice system and social services. But I found the insights and tools they offered were limited, and in some cases thought them more likely to compound harms than address them, bound as they are in the silence-punishment binary.

I began to look for people and groups who had developed alternatives. I learned about the paradigm-shifting approach of the Indigenous peoples and First Nations of North America (Turtle Island[4]), whose frameworks make up the heart of what we now know as restorative justice, a response to harm that works to repair the relationships shattered by it. That approach has in turn inspired models by both Christian congregations and anarchist collectives, which offered their own insights. I read also of contributions made by the Quakers,[5] the Māori,[6] and members of the Black Power movement. Most importantly, I discovered INCITE!, a network of radical feminists of color whose influence continues to resonate in anti-violence work.

I buttressed what I was learning about these frameworks with the findings and case studies of researchers and clinicians working to understand and treat the impact of trauma on the body and the mind. On that particular leg of my journey, I discovered the work of Stephen W. Porges, Peter Levine, Babette Rothschild, Laurie Leitch, and Bessel van der Kolk,[7] among others.

....

4   Turtle Island is the name the Iroquois, Anishinaabe, and other First Nations gave North America.

5   A historically Christian, abolitionist, and prison-reformist autonomous group.

6   A pan-tribal term that describes the people indigenous to New Zealand (Aotearoa).

7   As one of my sensitivity critics, M'kali-Hashiki, noted during review, this list of experts who work on trauma is populated by researchers of white and Ashkenazi backgrounds, which shows a bias on my part that needs to be explicitly stated, as it may limit aspects of this work. It's also important to note that though science strives for objectivity, it does not exist in a social vacuum, and systemic bias and erasure often limit research.

Most importantly, I began to participate in efforts to confront harm in my professional communities and groups of friends. For the past three years, I've been actively involved in community interventions in a variety of roles—both supporting survivors, and helping people who harm examine and change their patterns. I have also been called to account for harm that I have done. I have had the privilege of receiving help from friends and members of my communities in working not only to witness and do repair with the person I harmed, but to begin the journey of examining the beliefs and patterns that drive my actions.

This book would not exist without that work, and that work would not have been possible without the enormous contributions of Indigenous and First Nations people, the Black Power movement, and the autonomous efforts of communities of color, many of which continue to refine and expand their frameworks for transformative justice. I am most indebted to Creative Interventions, which was developed by Mimi Kim, one of the founding members of INCITE! I am enriched by the dialogue INCITE! began, as well as the projects that the network continues to catalyze, foster, and inspire in this space. This dialogue is long, rich, and ongoing.

§

I've learned many lessons while confronting harm, including my own, but the single most important one is that, very often, people do nothing not because we don't care, but because we don't know *what* to do. Trapped within the binary of silence and punishment, we have a difficult time even imagining what else might be possible. But give us *something* to do—especially something we feel equipped to do—and that feeling of paralysis melts away.

That's what this book is for. That's what I mean by "disrupting the bystander." I want to disrupt the silence-punishment binary in favor of something that works. There is a lot you can do, whether the person you care about is the one who was harmed or the one who caused the harm, and you don't need any specialized training to do it.

As it turns out, the most important toolbox for this work is one that the vast majority of us already possess: the one that comes with being human.

A Note About Language

It never ceases to amaze me how much trouble we can get ourselves into when we don't make sure everyone involved in a dialogue knows what we mean by the words we're using. For example, there's a dramatic difference between the scientific and colloquial definitions of the word *theory*: in science, it refers to an explanation supported by repeated experiments, while in colloquial use it refers to a wild guess that may or may not turn out to be correct. So let's go over some of the words I use in this book, and what I mean by them.

Accountability: I use the word *accountability* to refer to a process that begins, but does not end, with owning up to an action (or lack of action), intentional or not, that harmed someone else. The steps in such a process vary depending on the harm, and may involve any number of people, from a small group to a whole community. The person who was harmed may or may not choose to participate in the process.

Sometimes people assume that an accountability process only happens when the harm is "big." I think accountability is a way of life. After all, if we flake out on a friend and then are unwilling to hold space for them when they point out our neglect, how are we to do the same for harms associated with traumatic stress?

Activation: When I talk about *activation*, I'm specifically referring to a body that is experiencing lack of safety and is either on its way to, or already in, survival response. The human body is believed to have at least four categories of survival response, and the best-known among them are *fight* and *flight*. Less well-known are *freeze*, which is sometimes broken up into two, and *fawn*, a cooperative response that relies on social engagement to reestablish safety. Activation doesn't always happen in the face of imminent physical danger. Sometimes we become activated because our body detects cues it registers as signs that we are unsafe. A person may experience activation relating to harm they lived through even years after the event. Sadly, when it comes to trauma, time doesn't heal. Only bodily safety and belonging can tend these injuries.

Containering: I turn nouns into verbs sometimes and *container* is one of them. I could use "containing," but that implies suppression and brings to mind a disease outbreak. I want to be careful about conjuring images of contagion when I'm talking about activation, because while it is true that we affect one another's autonomic nervous systems just by being around one another, quarantine is absolutely not an appropriate response[8] to activation. Isolation kills social mammals and I don't want to leave any room for confusion about what I mean when I talk about helping someone who is having trouble managing a survival response. I use "containering" because in psychotherapy, the container is a safe space where things can be shared safely and heard

8   Stuart Grassian, "Psychopathological effects of solitary confinement," *American Journal of Psychiatry* 140, no. 11 (1983): 1450-1454, doi: https://doi.org/10.1176/ajp.140.11.1450

non-judgmentally. Friends don't provide therapy, but we can and do create this kind of space for one another. In doing so, we not only hold space for those who come to us, but also help them to regulate, which is restorative for them and can be protective for others. For example, someone who harmed may retaliate against the person naming the harm if friends don't provide a container for the person who harmed where regulation is possible without collusion. Collusion doesn't mitigate the risk of retaliation, and all but ensures future harm.

Discernment: When I use the word *discernment*, I am referring to a skill that uses bodily awareness to consider our boundaries and refine our needs and limits.

Disrupting: Here in Silicon Valley, *disrupt* is probably one of the most overused buzzwords of all time. We want to disrupt everything: dating, driving, eating—you name it. Clearly most of us could stand to watch the original *Jurassic Park* a few times until the core message[9] really sinks in, but the term's very overuse also made it an amusing and relatable way for me to describe getting people involved in confronting harm.

Flashback: When I use the word *flashback*, I'm referring specifically to the sensory experience that someone who has

---

9   Best summarized by the character Dr. Ian Malcolm, played by Jeff Goldblum: "Your scientists were so preoccupied with whether or not they *could*, they didn't stop to think if they *should*."

lived through trauma may have when they are triggered. A flashback may be auditory, olfactory, emotional, or otherwise felt in the body. Not all flashbacks completely recall or are directly related to the original event. Additionally, a person may not necessarily be aware that they're experiencing a flashback. As the body-focused psychotherapist and author Babette Rothschild points out, "Instances of hyperarousal, hyper-startle reflex, otherwise unexplainable emotional upset, physical pain, or intense irritation may all be easily explained by the phenomenon of flashback."[10]

Harm: If you hate my use of the word *harm*, you're not alone. People who read early drafts of this book universally agreed with you. "Harm" felt vague and euphemistic, they told me. I don't disagree, and I am certainly not encouraging you or anyone else to adopt this usage. I use this word with intent: I want this book to be as accessible to as many people as possible, and that means avoiding words that describe violence, which can be activating to some people. Activation and lack of safety make it difficult to learn and take in information.[11] In my experience, the people most likely to show up to confront violence in communities are other survivors, so it is important for me to take care to minimize accidental exposure to such language.

....

10   Babette Rothschild, *The Body Remembers: The Psychophysiology of Trauma and Trauma Recovery* (New York: W.W. Norton & Company, 2000).
11   Bessel van der Kolk, *The Body Keeps the Score: Brain, Mind, and Body in the Healing of Trauma* (New York: Penguin Books, 2015).

Holding space: I use the phrase *holding space* to refer to the act of being present for another person to witness, validate, and support them as they experience and explore their changing cognitive, emotional, and physiological states. A key goal of holding space is not to create any action items for the other person, either by telling them what they should do about the situation or by requiring them to manage our own emotional state.

Intervention: I use the word *intervention* to refer to any attempt by an individual or a group to stop harm from happening or continuing to happen. An intervention may be as simple as interrupting a single interaction, and as complex as gathering a group to confront a mutual friend about harmful or worrying behavior.

Owning: I use the verb *owning* as shorthand for "owning up," or acknowledging that one did harm. For example, "the first step of accountability is owning" or "you need to own the harm." A similar shorthand is *naming*, which is short for "naming the harm," or verbalizing the harm. For example, "naming is the first step out of the fog," or "things change when you start to name." Note that naming always refers to the harm and may not involve disclosing the identity of the person who harmed.

Person who harmed: I don't love this term, but in doing accountability work with others, I have come to deeply recognize the value of separating *who we are* from *what* *we do.* If we refer to a person as a "harm-er" or "harm-ist," we think of them as a person defined by harm, whereas a "person who harmed" is a person who did harm, but who may choose to become a person who seeks to be accountable, and to change. I learned this phrase from Creative Interventions, a resource center dedicated to creating and promoting community-based resources to end violence, which adopted it as an alternative to criminalizing language like *perpetrator* and *offender*—both of which reflect and reinforce the silence-punishment binary.

Pod: The Bay Area Transformative Justice Collective coined the word *pod* to describe "the people that you would call on if harm happened to you; or the people that you would call on if you wanted support in taking accountability for harm that you've done; or if you witnessed harm or if someone you care about was harming or being harmed."

Pods can be large or small. The *support pod* is the group that provides support to a survivor, and the *accountability pod* is the group that helps the person who harmed with their accountability. *Pod work* is any activity undertaken as part of a pod. *Podding* is sometimes used as shorthand for "being in a pod."

A survivor may form a pod to receive support after harm without calling on the person who harmed to do accountability, or even disclosing who they are (if they know their identity). In such situations, there is only one pod. Likewise, a person who notices or suspects that they have a pattern of harm may convene a pod to help them examine their actions without necessarily involving the person or people they harmed.

Regulation: When I use the word *regulation*, I mean the process by which humans modulate our emotional responses, including our response to threat. Most humans are capable of helping one another regulate by being social, an activity that allows us to give and receive signals of safety and belonging using our bodies (attention, eye contact, tone of voice, facial expression, etc.).[12] Not every human is capable of issuing or registering every kind of safety cue. When we regulate with others, the process is referred to as *interpersonal emotional regulation*, or *co-regulation*. When our emotional state gets destabilized, on the other hand, the word is *dysregulation*.

Safety: Behavioral neuroscientist Stephen W. Porges uses the word *safety* to describe not the removal of a threat, but the state of the body when it is not primed for defense.[13] This definition of safety informs my own. Though imminent threats do exist in many situations of harm, a large percentage of survivor support involves creating and fostering the conditions for a survivor's nervous system to come out of survival response and recalibrate their felt sense of safety. Bringing a nervous system out of activation is not a

....

12   Stephen W. Porges, *The Pocket Guide to the Polyvagal Theory: The Transformative Power of Feeling Safe* (New York: W.W. Norton & Company, 2017).
13   Porges, *The Pocket Guide to the Polyvagal Theory*.

conscious process, but rather a natural one that is facilitated by people gathering to support a survivor. Showing up—especially physically or in a technologically assisted way that involves the face and voice—improves a survivor's chances of returning to a physical state that supports connection, restoration, and health. We'll talk more about the role of others in recalibrating safety in this book.

Safety cues are the millions of data points bodies register in their assessment of safety, a process that uses *neuroception*. Bodies don't only register safety cues—they also issue them. The opposite of a safety cue is a *danger cue*. Our understanding of both types of cues is growing all the time.

Self-care: When I talk about *self-care*, I mean actions a person may take to improve or maintain a sense of well-being, which may involve activities to decrease their level of activation. What constitutes self-care varies from one person to the next. What makes one body happy may not do the same for another body. This is part of a longer conversation, but the key takeaway is: when someone tells us that meditation or working out doesn't help them, let's believe them instead of insisting or assuming they don't want to help themselves.

Shelter: When I use the term *shelter*, I refer to the act of finding safety together. I recognize that for many people, the term has negative connotations (i.e., leading a sheltered life with little experience of the world). I am sorry for the way this beautiful word has evolved in meaning! Please know that by its use I do not mean to imply that people supporting a survivor should isolate the survivor from the community, or that they should keep information from a survivor.

Survivor: I use the word *survivor* to refer to an individual who has experienced harm. I use it instead of *victim* for the same reason that I avoid "perpetrator" and "offender": I don't want to conjure or reinforce the silence-punishment binary.

In addition, I dislike the way the word *victim* redefines someone who has experienced a harm by that experience. Our experiences of harm impact us, but they do not define us. *Survivor* refocuses the attention on the human and their resilience. It is a word in motion, one that to me describes a person overcoming the harm, the silence, the disclosure, the aftermath, and the integration journey that follows.

Not everyone who has experienced harm prefers to use this word to describe themselves. When interacting with people who have experienced harm or other adverse events, it is important to ask what label they prefer (and, unless explicitly asked, not to lecture them on why you don't agree with their choice!).

Support: I use the word *support* to describe any help, assistance, or action taken to aid people involved in an intervention, whether it's for the survivor or the person who harmed. The roles for those helping a person who harmed are different from the ones for those helping someone who was harmed, but they also overlap: for instance, helping the person who harmed regulate their emotional responses, making sure they are engaging in self-care as they undertake the work of accountability, and so on.

Transformative justice: When I talk about *transformative justice*, I use the definition articulated in the generationFIVE white paper *Toward Transformative Justice*: "the dual process of securing individual justice while transforming structures of social injustice"[14] that allow and enable harm to occur.

Trigger: The word *trigger* has passed into colloquial usage to describe anything upsetting or angering. Because of this, I try not to use the word too much, but when I do, I am referring to anything capable of causing a survival response or flashback in a person with trauma. Survival responses or flashbacks can happen whether or not someone's aware of the trauma or of all their triggers.

Triggers can relate to any of the five senses, as well any number of other senses most able-bodied people don't generally think about, such as proprioception, the sense of where and how our body is in space, which includes our posture.

----

14   generationFIVE, "Toward Transformative Justice: A Liberatory Approach to Child Sexual Abuse and other forms of Intimate and Community Violence". June 2007. http://www.generationfive.org/wp-content/uploads/2013/07/G5_Toward_Transformative_Justice-Document.pdf

A Reminder to You

As you read this book, you may recall or realize that in trying to help others, you've done or said things that did more harm than good. There is courage in looking at your past this way, but I also want you to remember that you were doing the best you could with what you knew at the time.

In 2018, Carmen Leilani De Jesus, administrator at the School of Consent, taught me something revolutionary: I could forgive myself for previous gaps in my knowledge. I invite you to do that for yourself now. Say: "I forgive myself for any gaps in my knowledge." Forgiving ourselves makes it possible to take in the lessons presented by our mistakes. Most importantly, it enables us to approach those we hurt with the openness that makes repair possible.

We're not born knowing how to respond to crisis, and we don't exist in a society that teaches us how to make use of the gifts that come from being social mammals. Those among us who develop the skills to care well for ourselves and others eventually get there through experience, but no one's experience is without mistakes.

The mistakes we make have a lot to teach us. Earlier I mentioned two mistakes I made before I started this journey, describing them as goslings that follow me around. This reframing of mistakes into goslings is intentional. Making mistakes is scary for a lot of us, and this sometimes prevents us from taking action altogether or from owning the harm that results when we do make a mistake. In turning mistakes into goslings, I alchemized a terrifying thing into a sweet creature worthy of tending. And it is in this tending that we do our learning.

You would not believe the gaggle I've hatched while doing this work—and there'll be more! You can't embrace the belief that we never stop learning without also accepting that we will continue to make mistakes along the way. So let's welcome our goslings—not with shame and criticism founded on unreasonable expectations of ourselves, but with gentleness. They are here to teach us.

Remember: The measure of a person is not in whether they are perfect, but in how they choose to act when they discover they've made a mistake or hurt someone else.

Part 1: When Someone You Know Was Harmed

Chapter 1: Remember the Human

Being present for a person who has been harmed is without question one of the most important aspects of intervening in harm. As social mammals, we depend on others for regulation and sheltering. The isolation that many survivors experience, then, is not only unfortunate but harmful, as it actively undermines their ability to regulate.

American movies and television shows are full of fantasies of justice[15] in which a regular guy or gal decides they've had enough of an injustice and heads out to save the day. They're called fantasies of justice for a reason: in our society, the prevailing idea is that regular people like you and me are not capable of responding to harm on our own. We're taught that we need someone in a position of authority to step in when harm happens—law enforcement, social services, human resources, and so on. The less we

....

15   This term was coined by Lois McMaster Bujold in a speech at Denvention 3 in 2008. Find the full text here: http://dendarii.com/denver08.html

regular people meddle, we're told, the better for the person who experienced the harm.

And yet many people who experience harm and interact with the systems currently in place to address it find them to be not only lacking, but alienating and dehumanizing. A 2003 Ms. Foundation report[16] concluded that the criminal justice system offers inaccessible, disempowering, and even harmful solutions to women and children survivors. Those who experience harm in the workplace fare no better: in 2016, a United States Equal Employment Opportunity Commission Select Task Force[17] concluded that taking formal action is the least likely option chosen by men and women who experience harm at work. Employees avoid reporting, the authors note, "because they anticipate and fear a number of reactions—disbelief of their claim; inaction on their claim; receipt of blame for causing the offending actions; social retaliation (including humiliation and os-tracism); and professional retaliation, such as damage to their career and reputation." Citing other studies, the report concluded that these fears are well founded.

The same report also found that the action most likely to be taken by those who'd experienced harm is to reach out to trusted others for support. Among women who had

....

16   Ms. Foundation for Women. "Safety & Justice for All: Safety Program: Examining the Relationship Between the Women's Movement and the Criminal Legal System," 2003.
http://www.ncdsv.org/images/Ms_SafetyJusticeForAll_2003.pdf
17   Equal Employment Opportunity Commission. "EEOC Select Task Force on the Study of Harassment in the Workplace," 2016.
https://www.eeoc.gov/eeoc/task_force/harassment/report.
cfm#_Toc453686303

experienced harm, 27 to 37 percent reached out to family members, and 50 to 70 percent sought support from friends.

When we evaluate the actions taken by survivors of harm, we often create a mental hierarchy in which we place authority figures at the top and trusted people closer to the bottom. This hierarchy becomes a lens, so when we look at the conclusions of reports like that of the Select Task Force, we assume that workers who experience harm turn to family and friends because the formal channels are risky, ineffective, or inaccessible. We imagine that if the formal channels were improved, workers would choose them instead.

But what if that's not the whole picture? What if there is a purpose in reaching out to trusted others? What if survivors of harm are turning to people they trust because humans are social mammals, and taking shelter in one another is how we as social mammals evolved to stabilize our nervous systems in the aftermath of harm?

§

In the '90s, we had something called "netiquette": a set of basic norms for interacting online. The first rule, as codified by Virginia Shea,[18] was "Remember the human." This rule asked those who were getting on internet forums for the first time to keep in mind that they were interacting with other human beings, even if they couldn't see them. Times have changed, and the culture of the internet with them, but the rule continues to have resonance for me. And as technology

18   Virginia Shea, *Netiquette* (San Francisco, CA: Albion Books, 1994). Available online at www.albion.com/netiquette/book/index.html

continues to advance—taking us further away from each other and our bodies—it feels more important than ever.

We cannot forget the human, not only in others, but in ourselves. We're social mammals: we come equipped with sophisticated detection systems, internal dashboards, intelligent response protocols, and networking capabilities. We are the most elegant machines we will ever behold, capable of stabilizing not only ourselves, but one another.

When we interact, our bodies register a million little cues through a process called neuroception[19] which lets our nervous systems know if we're under threat. It's safe to say that not all bodies are capable of registering all cues, though we haven't catalogued all cues that human neuroception responds to. We know that the tone, pitch, and timbre of our voices are cues—as are the arches and furrows of our brows, the softness of our looks, the direction taken by the corners of our mouths, the tilt of our heads, and other aspects of our postures. The word "neuroception" may be new, but what it describes is common enough to the human experience to have collected many names over time: inkling, gut feeling, witchy vibes, women's intuition, energy, instinct, the sixth sense. Our bodies are able to pick up so many cues in so little time that it can feel like magic, especially when it helps us avoid a dangerous person or risky situation. But it's not magic—it's just one aspect of inhabiting the awe-inspiring machine that is our body.

....

19   Stephen W. Porges, *The Polyvagal Theory: Neurophysiological Foundations of Emotions, Attachment, Communication, and Self-regulation* (New York: W.W. Norton & Company, 2011).

This same mechanism that gauges safety in any given situation is also involved in how we relate to one another. We evolved to connect with others, and our nervous systems routinely bridge the space between our bodies, sending and receiving information through numerous cues. These cues inform the way we respond to those we're engaging with, and they are capable of shifting our internal states. Just as interacting with someone who's in a bad mood can put us in a bad mood as well, being met by someone with compassion can shift our distress toward calm.

A shift in state from calm to activation (see "A Note About Language" in the Introduction) is called *dysregulation*, and it tends to happen when we don't have the emotional bandwidth or inner resources to cope when things go wrong or we engage someone who is activated. A shift in the opposite direction is called *regulation*. When we have the emotional bandwidth and internal resources to cope, most of us are able to shift this way on our own (*self-regulation*), but very often, we rely on others (*co-regulation*)[20].

Helping someone regulate doesn't require that we solve their problems—it only requires that we meet them in their distress calmly and openly. This is not always easy to do, but if you are a social mammal who interacts with at least a handful of other social mammals in your life, you have already done it. As you read the next sections of this book, you'll begin to see just how deeply you already grasp much of this concept.

....

20   Jamil Zaki and W. Craig Williams, "Interpersonal emotion regulation," *Emotion* 13, no. 5. (Oct. 2013): 803-810. http://psycnet.apa. org/doiLanding?doi=10.1037%2Fa0033839

We're not taught useful things about responding to interpersonal harm and it will take time to fully deprogram what hasn't served us in the past and what allows harm to continue in our communities. It will feel overwhelming, but the most important thing is that the capacity to help others regulate *is something you already carry*. In this section, I'll go over how you can reinforce safety cues and minimize danger cues while responding to a survivor.

Setting Priorities: Shift, Shelter, and Shape

Few things are unmanageable if we break them into smaller pieces we can tackle one at a time. From first aid to site reliability engineering, breaking up a crisis into smaller bits not only makes anything less daunting, it makes it easier to recruit others to help. Most importantly, it gives us an idea of what tasks need doing and which ones take priority.

Prioritizing is crucial in a crisis, whether you're dealing with an injury, service outage, or harm. In first aid, if a person is found unconscious, the first thing we do after making sure there's no ongoing threat is to check that they're breathing. If they're not, we don't stop to diagnose what might have happened to them—we immediately open the airway and begin CPR. Similarly, when there's a service outage, the first priority in site reliability engineering is to get a system to some basic level of functionality before diving in to look for the cause of the problem.

Survivor support also has priorities. The first one, which I call *Shift*, is the process we talked about in the section on regulation: helping someone in distress reach a greater calm. The second priority is *Shelter*, which involves rallying others to reintegrate a survivor. And finally, there is *Shape*: letting the survivor determine what form their future may take.

Shift

You can't *make* someone feel safe, but you can help *shift* their nervous system out of activation. This is crucial to helping someone return to a sense of internal safety. Shifting someone is the single most important task in survivor support, and it takes priority whenever the survivor gets activated. Activation not only happens immediately after an incident of harm, but may flare up at any time—even years later.

Addressing immediate needs or completing task items may be required before a survivor's plate is sufficiently clear for them to recalibrate safety, so on occasion logistics and short-term planning will come into play during Shift. For the most part, however, Shift is primarily relational.

Shelter

It only takes one person to break the isolation of harm and help us begin to regulate, but nothing is more restorative to our internal sense of safety than having more people show up. One person can Shift, but several can *Shelter*. Calling on friends and other trusted people in a survivor's life means more hands to take care of things. And more means more—more skill sets, more knowledge, and more load-balancing. Balancing the load is crucial to helping a survivor regulate, as no one's internal resources are infinite, especially when we're providing care. We all need to recharge, and to do that, we need to know the survivor is in good hands.

***

Shape

Shift and Shelter are about helping a survivor regain the internal resources that are depleted by living through and coping with harm—they're about restoration. *Shape*, on the other hand, is about transformation. Shape has planning at its center. It asks the question, "what can make things better?" This question may orient efforts outward toward the person who harmed and the wider community, but it doesn't have to. A survivor could, for instance, choose to call for accountability from the person who harmed them, or from people in the community who did nothing when harm was happening, or both. Or Shape could play out less publicly, such as in the case of a survivor who decides they want to leave a living situation with someone harming them. In Shape, those providing support will help a survivor define their goals, go over their options, take stock of the risks, and help get things in motion.

Things don't always unfold in a way that favors this order or priority. Sometimes we show up and cops are already there. Other times, a survivor comes to us when they have already decided to leave a relationship where harm is happening. In these cases, we are called to do a little bit of everything at the same time. This isn't impossible, but it's a lot more challenging.

When Tarana Burke founded the Me Too movement[21] in 2006, her intention was to help survivors of harm break out of isolation and shame by connecting with one another. This focus on connection was altered when the actress Alyssa Milano turned the words into a viral campaign eleven years later.[22] By making disclosure a political act, #metoo refocused the intent of Me Too from Shift to Shape. While #metoo as a whole has been and remains an agent of change, many individual survivors who have come forward without support have paid heavy personal costs.

Survivors who name harm through a callout without having established a connection with even one person in their physical lives who can help them regulate are often brutalized by the ordeal of coming forward. It's not easy to help someone regulate while their experience of harm is being debated. The best-case scenario is one where by-standers who witness the disclosure rally to offer support

21   Sandra E. Garcia, "The Woman Who Created #MeToo Long Before Hashtags." *The New York Times*, Oct. 20, 2017. https://www.nytimes.com/2017/10/20/us/me-too-movement-tarana-burke.html

22   Alyssa Milano (@alyssa_milano), Twitter, October 15, 2017, 1:21 p.m., https://twitter.com/alyssa_milano/status/919659438700670976

to a survivor, but even this can feel terrifying to someone whose embodied sense of safety hasn't been reestablished.

I don't regret #metoo. I regret that many survivors step forward without support, and that many still remain unsheltered.

Body Talk

To understand why the priority levels are necessary, we need to talk a little bit about the human body. When a person is in distress, their nervous system jumps into action to ensure survival. Most of us are familiar with two responses to danger: fight and flight. The jury is still out on how many different responses there are, or whether they are distinct responses or a continuum, but one model I've found extremely useful in responding to harm is the Sextuple ANS Theory[23] developed by the psychotherapist and trauma specialist Babette Rothschild. This model understands autonomic nervous system (or ANS) response as a spectrum. To keep things brief, I'll primarily focus on the model's three responses to threat, which Rothschild calls fight/flight, hyperfreeze, and hypofreeze (or collapse). I'll also mention another response called fawn,[24] or "tend and

23   Babette Rothschild, *The Body Remembers, Volume 2: Revolutionizing Trauma Treatment* (New York: W.W. Norton & Company, 2017).
24   Pete Walker, *Complex PTSD: From Surviving to Thriving: A Guide and Map for Recovering from Childhood Trauma* (California: Azure Coyote Publishing, 2013).

befriend," which is not part of Rothschild's model but is relevant to this discussion.

Responding to a threat is a full-body process. It involves our senses, our organ function, our blood pressure, our brain, our breathing, our muscle tension—everything. When we register danger and our body prepares to respond, we go on high alert, looking for signs that *confirm* danger. This means our body will prefer to err on the side of caution, such as by reading neutral faces as angry.[25] And that, in turn, means that spaces full of danger cues like hospitals, clinics, and police departments may push a survivor over the edge. What "over the edge" means is variable, as you'll see.

When a person is in fight/flight, decisions that fall outside of their body's single goal of reestablishing internal safety are not prioritized. Even when a survivor agrees that it's a good idea for a doctor to take a look at an injury, they may not be able to remain calm or stay in the hospital long enough for that to happen. Their brain's prefrontal cortex— which is necessary to make sound long-term decisions—may not be online. Their ability to engage with others while in this state is also limited, though it is possible if they receive enough safety cues.

A person in hyperfreeze is like a deer in the headlights, locked in a state of muscular rigidity until an opportunity to escape presents itself. In this state, their pupils tend to be dilated, their breathing is fast and shallow, and their heart rate is elevated. The prefrontal cortex is not likely to

....

25   Deb Dana, *The Polyvagal Theory in Therapy: Engaging the Rhythm of Regulation* (New York: W.W. Norton & Company, 2018).

be online, and dissociation (a state of disconnection from the here and now) is possible. Connecting with others is unlikely in this state. "They may be able to answer questions," writes Rothschild, "but thinking will not be clear. In this situation, the best response is to slam on the brakes. That is, do whatever you can to reduce stress and provocation."

Hypofreeze, in contrast, is a full-system numbing, as though the body has determined that the threat is impossible to fight or flee, and the end is imminent. The breath and heart both slow in this state, the stare becomes vacant, the muscles go limp, and the posture collapses on itself. The prefrontal cortex is not online in this state, dissociation is highly likely, and connection is impossible. When a survivor hypofreezes, the best course of action is to provide small comforts such as a glass of water and a blanket, and to reduce other sources of stimulation. Rothschild likens this type of freeze to a computer crash: "Neither of these situations (human or computer) will be eased by increasing activity, load, or charge." However, if someone you perceive to be in a freeze state faints and their muscles are flaccid, check their pulse. If they're not conscious and their pulse is slow, you might have to call for medical help.

Finally, there's the fawn response, which relies on social engagement and cooperation to recalibrate safety. This is an incredibly sophisticated response to threat that we're only just beginning to understand. When people say that natural disasters bring out the best in humanity, they're talking about fawn. That makes it easy to think that it wouldn't be much of a problem if a survivor went into fawn at the hospital—what doctor doesn't want a cooperative patient? But fawn has a shadow side that can seriously complicate consent—as in Stockholm Syndrome, or when a survivor cooks breakfast for the person who harmed them the morning after the harm. There is a lot we still don't know about the way fawn plays out in the body, but its impact on consent is why I have to include it here. Fawn is one more reason we must be careful not to push a survivor to make big decisions when they're activated, and why we must be understanding and patient even if they appear changeable and inconsistent. (This doesn't mean you should discourage them from doing anything "just in case" they're in fawn or question them about their decisions. But we'll talk more about dos and don'ts in a bit.)

Heart Rate

You can check someone's heart rate by putting two fingers on the side of the windpipe or over the radial artery, which travels down the thumb side of the wrist. Once you locate the pulse, set a timer on your phone for 15 seconds and count the number of beats you feel. Multiply that number by four to calculate the number of beats per minute. A normal resting heart rate for adults ranges from 60 to 100 beats per minute, though some athletes can have a resting heart rate as low as 40.[26]

26   American Heart Association, "Know Your Target Heart Rates for Exercise, Losing Weight and Health." http://www.heart.org/en/healthy-living/fitness/fitness-basics/target-heart-rates

When we think of survival responses, we tend to imagine the threats that cause them as clear and present physical dangers, something we might see on a nature documentary. But threats are not always this obvious. Our body may even read insufficient safety cues as a serious threat. Its assessment of safety is very context-dependent, and a big part of this context is our existing level of activation: if we're already primed for defense, our body is going to focus on identifying signals that confirm the danger is ongoing so that we're not caught unprepared. That means that when a friend's nervous system is engaged in threat response and ours isn't, it can be like we each occupy a different reality despite being in the same place. It's not that they're wrong or over-reacting: their bodies are right to read many environments and situations in the modern city as terrifying. Stephen W. Porges, a behavioral neuroscientist who researches the internal sense of safety, estimates that hospitals and similar societal institutions are as likely to trigger feelings of danger in the body as war and political unrest.[27] We don't share our friend's terror not because there's nothing to be afraid of but because we are not looking for confirmation of danger. Unlike them, our bodies are prioritizing safety cues, and have the bandwidth to cope with any danger cues that do get through. This is why trying to convince someone that it's safe doesn't work: their body does not feel it's safe, and you can't argue with a body. In fact, arguing may overload an already overburdened system and push them into a more extreme response.

....

27   Porges, *The Pocket Guide to the Polyvagal Theory.*

If you've ever wondered why someone who was harmed would take a shower, wash their clothes, burn their sheets, or otherwise do away with what you view as "evidence," there's your answer: the scent and remnants of someone who harmed them are danger cues, and allowing these cues to remain is incompatible with returning to an internal state of safety. It may not make sense in the context of what we're told we need to do to get "justice," but for as long as I've been helping people through crisis, I've found that the fastest way back to a restored internal sense of safety is to trust a survivor's body in its assessment of danger. If they don't want to leave their house, if they don't want to go to a clinic to get tested, if they don't want to file a police report, if they don't want any part of their body examined or swabbed, if they don't want to tell you what happened, *don't make them.*

As I mentioned earlier, there are going to be situations where you don't have time to help someone shift out of activation before you have to go somewhere or do something else. Sometimes, by the time you show up, the cops are already there. Other times, the injuries require immediate medical attention. We work with what we have, and we do the best we can.

But if you do have time to help someone shift, *take it.*

Chapter 2: Shift

Shifting is about signaling safety to a body. By staying calm and rooted in openness and compassion, we naturally generate the physical cues that signal to another person's body that they're safe. It can be difficult to trust that we're capable of doing this because we don't place a lot of importance on body language in our society, and many of us don't think or know much about it. But body language is the primary language of safety cues, so before we dive into tips on how to listen and what to say, let's talk a little bit about these cues, both the ones that we give with our bodies and the ones in our environment. As you read, keep in mind that there are far more safety cues than those listed here, and that this field of research is still emerging. In addition, remember that not all bodies can generate or receive all the cues listed here, but that does not mean that they are incapable of shifting or being shifted.

The most important cue you can give is your attention. Betty Martin, the cofounder of the School of Consent, refers to attention as a gift we can give to others. I want you to think about your own attention in this way. A gift is offered—it is not imposed. Give your attention to the survivor with soft eyes, and don't hold expectations about their response. They may not hold your gaze. That's okay—gaze-averting is a common trauma adaptation. They may look at their hands some of the time, and then around the room as their nervous system stabilizes. Let it happen. Continue to give your attention and provide the cues of safety that your body already knows how to provide, such as leaning in their direction or slightly tilting your head to hear them better, occasionally nodding and making small sounds to indicate you're still following what they're saying.

If this is hard for you—for example, some of us struggle with social anxiety, have trouble making eye contact, or have difficulty listening to hard things in general—gently let a survivor know. You don't need to go into detail about what's going on for you. You can simply say something like "I'm fully present with you, but it's hard for me to maintain eye contact for a long time."

"The muscles of the face and head provide cues that the other is safe to approach," says Stephen W. Porges. "How we look at each other is a critical feature of this capacity to connect. Subtle cues of understanding, of shared feelings, and of intent are conveyed."[28]

You've probably had the experience being asked "what are you thinking?" or "where did you go?" while in a conversation where you've drifted away, staring off into space or out the window. This kind of shift in attention is

28   Porges, *The Pocket Guide to the Polyvagal Theory.*

something that our nervous systems have evolved to recognize. Questions like these are the biological equivalent of a dialog box popping up on a computer to let us know we've lost internet connectivity: repair connection or work offline? The adaptive social mammal will always attempt to repair the connection unless danger cues overwhelm them.

When we're in distress, it takes little to overwhelm us. Even too few safety cues can cause us to pull back. If you've ever felt put off by someone answering a text in the middle of the conversation, you've experienced what Porges refers to as "biological rudeness," which is when one nervous system registers disconnection from another. "Sorry, it's work," the person we were speaking with may say as they frantically type into their phone, their eyes glued to the screen. We may intellectually understand that it's not personal, but it doesn't matter. Our nervous systems aren't concerned with whether or not it's personal, only with whether or not we're still connected. As Deb Dana, clinician and coordinator of the Kinsey Institute Traumatic Stress Research Consortium, puts it, "Our common human experience is to feel soothed in the presence of others and distressed when we are left behind."[29]

When we're not in distress, we are able to move through these disconnections with an ease that is simply not available to us when we are. Connection is more of a lifeline than ever when we are in distress, but it is also more fragile and tricky to repair. This doesn't mean that you can't pause to make tea, or get a blanket if the survivor needs it—but

....

29   Dana, *The Polyvagal Theory in Therapy.*

check in with them first about whether whatever you're thinking about doing is helpful for them. Do they *want* tea? Also, consider alternatives: do they need a blanket from the next room, or can you throw your coat over them for now? Survivor support calls on us to be the ones to initiate connection repair and to safeguard that connection as we work to reduce the load on a survivor's nervous system.

"Biological rudeness is a cascade, which starts with a lack of reciprocity to a spontaneous social engagement that triggers an autonomic state of defense, and ends with an emotional response of being offended that may lead to an aggressive reaction," says Porges. "It's really quite amazing how easily our body changes states when someone disengages or engages with us."[30]

If you fiddle, tap your fingers or feet, shake your leg, or have another "nervous" habit, it might be helpful to let a survivor know that this is something you do to soothe yourself and it should not be interpreted as impatience. Even more helpful would be to use that opportunity to issue a reconnection request, such as by making eye contact and saying, "I do that when I'm nervous, and I am filled with anxiety listening to what you went through, but *I am here for you*. I am taking care of myself and I will be okay. Is there anything we can do right now to make you more comfortable or help you take care of yourself?"

Another important sense in detecting safety or threat is hearing. A nervous system that has moved into defense is listening for very different things in the environment than

....

30   Porges, *The Pocket Guide to the Polyvagal Theory*.

one that is not. Safety cues prime our ear structures to listen to human voices, whereas danger cues give precedence to the sounds our bodies associate with danger. Danger cues are unfortunately very common in the modern city, which came into being before we realized the impact of low-frequency sounds. Ventilators, heaters, refrigerators, air filtration systems, trains, airplanes, and other mechanical vibrations that propagate over the ground and through walls can be extremely dysregulating to the nervous system.[31] This has three notable consequences for survivors: one, it makes much of the modern world intolerable. Two, it makes connecting with us through talk more challenging because a survivor's body is prioritizing sounds and vibrations that confirm danger over human voices. And three, the discrepancy between a survivor's reactions and our body's own assessment of danger can make it difficult to relate and maintain a connection. This incongruity can be tricky to navigate, but it also means that we have more resources to work with. As long as we don't dismiss the fear or anxiety a survivor is feeling, we can use our body's prioritizing of voices to remain calm and help the survivor shift.

It's not easy to find places in a modern city or town that are free of low-frequency sounds and vibrations, but you can reduce such cues by turning off any likely sources in your immediate area, such as air-purifying units or space

....

31   H. Findeis and E. Peters, "Disturbing Effects of Low Frequency Sound Immissions and Vibrations in Residential Buildings," *Noise Health* 6, no. 23 (2004): 29-35, http://www.noiseandhealth.org/article.asp?issn=1463-1741;year=2004;volume=6;issue=23;spage=29;epage=35;aulast=Findeis

heaters. If you absolutely must seek medical attention, consider that a hospital will be full of low-frequency sounds (and other potentially frightening cues), and do your best to shift the survivor with safety cues before you head there.

Keep in mind that although an activated nervous system will be listening for danger cues, it will still recognize safety if enough cues present themselves. A survivor may not be able to focus and fully participate in a conversation, but you can meet them where they're at by using your attention and your voice to provide enough safety cues to help them begin to shift. Since our voices provide a smorgasbord of cues to a listener's nervous system, signaling our emotional state and letting them know whether or not it's safe to approach, you can use your voice to do the bulk of the work. Most of us already know how to do this and regularly do through the use of *prosody*, the rhythm and range of a person's pitch in speech. The way some adults speak to babies and domestic animals is an excellent illustration of prosodic voice with an emphasis on higher notes. We may not speak to other adults that way, but we do employ variations in pitch all the time—it's hard to connect with others in a monotone voice!

There are many other known voice cues. *Tempo* is the speed with which we speak, and it tends to slow when we are soothing another person. *Timbre* describes the overtones that give each note a texture, like breathiness, nasality, or twang. Lastly, *attack* refers to how sharply we begin sounds and hit consonants. When we try to speak more clearly, projecting our voice from the chest and enunciating better, we deepen our voices, reduce prosody, and hit consonants more sharply, which undermines many safety cues made possible by speech. You intuitively understand this—you wouldn't try to soothe someone who is going through a hard time the same way you'd give a TED Talk.

"When we detect prosodic voices, the neural response to those sounds changes our physiological state," Porges says. "When we listen to intonation—prosodic features of voice—we are reading the other person's physiological state. If the physiological state is calm, it is reflected in a melodic voice, and listening to that voice calms us down. Another way of thinking about the relations between vocalizations and listening is to understand that long before there was syntax or language in mammals, there were vocalizations, and vocalizations were an important component of social interaction."[32]

Music has charms to soothe

Preliminary research suggests that it may be possible to shift someone from a state of defense to one of social engagement using recorded media,[33] though the mechanism through which this process works is not yet well understood. An intervention developed by Porges called the Safe and Sound Protocol[34] uses the vocalizations of

32   Porges, *The Pocket Guide to the Polyvagal Theory.*
33   Stephen W. Porges et al., "Reducing Auditory Hypersensitivities in Autistic Spectrum Disorder: Preliminary Findings Evaluating the Listening Project Protocol," *Frontiers in Pediatrics* 2, 2014: 80, doi: 10.3389/fped.2014.00080
34   "The Safe and Sound Protocol," Integrated Listening Systems, 2018, https://integratedlistening.com/ssp-safe-sound-protocol/

female performers that have been altered to exaggerate prosody.

Another set of important safety cues relate to bodily comfort. The autonomic nervous system is deeply involved in temperature regulation, so providing assistance with a warm blanket, a drink, or some other simple intervention can help a body begin to stabilize. Warmth also helps release tense muscles, while soft surfaces are comforting for a loose posture. Some people may find it comforting to remain in a quiet room, while others may seek out more natural surroundings. There seems to be greater variation here than with other cues, likely because increasing bodily comfort is so much more contextual. Weighted blankets are a great example. Based on a self-soothing intervention developed by the autism activist and Colorado State University animal science professor Temple Grandin,[35] weighted blankets contain pockets of sand-like material that replicate a feeling of being hugged. This uniform, full-body sensation can be deeply soothing for those with sensory hypersensitivities, while to a body primed for a flight response, the weight can feel extremely alarming.

The key with external cues is to remember that you can co-create with the survivor the comfort they need to stabilize. You can ask if they want a blanket, if they want a pillow,

....

35   Temple Grandin, "Calming Effects of Deep Touch Pressure in Patients with Autistic Disorder, College Students, and Animals," *Journal of Child and Adolescent Psychopharmacology* 2, no. 1 (1992): 63-72, http://www.grandin.com/inc/squeeze.html

if they want to dim or brighten the lights. You don't have to know everything—no one knows everything.

Shifting is never really finished, which is why I don't think about it as a step so much as a priority, something to be done whenever a survivor needs it. Many things can dysregulate someone who is grappling with an experience of harm, because simply coping is taking up so much of their bandwidth. Tread gently and with understanding, and remember that you already carry within you the tools you need to help others.

How immediately do you have to do things?

The morning-after pill and post-exposure prophylaxis (or PEP, a short-term antiretroviral therapy one can take to reduce the likelihood of contracting HIV) can be taken up to 72 hours after contact. A copper IUD can work as emergency contraception up to five days after contact.[36]

In the United States, a survivor can choose to have what is called an unreported medical forensic exam[37] (or Jane/John Doe kit). These exams collect evidence of harm in case a survivor eventually decides to report, and they are viewed as a middle ground between immediately going to police and not reporting.

36   Bliss Kaneshiro and Tod Aeby, "Long-Term Safety, Efficacy, and Patient Acceptability of the Intrauterine Copper T-380A Contraceptive Device," *International Journal of Women's Health* 2 (2010): 211-220, https://www.ncbi.nlm.nih.gov/pmc/articles/PMC2971735/
37   National Center for Victims of Crime, "Unreported/ Anonymous Sexual Assault Kits," http://victimsofcrime.org/ our-programs/dna-resource-center/untested-sexual-assault-kits/ unreported-sexual-assault-kits

Note that some states require doctors to report "suspicious injuries" to law enforcement.

What to Say

Now that we have discussed how the body picks up cues and what some of these cues are, we can proceed to a more general discussion about what to say when someone tells you they experienced harm.

When I'm holding space for someone who is making a disclosure, I like to think of the idea of "the container." In psychotherapy, the container is a welcoming space in which things can be shared safely and heard non-judgmentally. Though peers like you and me don't provide therapy to a survivor, we do want to create a similar vibe. This begins with the safety cues we discussed earlier, and extends to saying things that strengthen and maintain our connection with a survivor. I learned a number of these tips from Creative Interventions, whose manual for intervening in harm, the *Creative Interventions Toolkit*,[38] is absolutely crucial reading for anyone doing survivor support.

The types of verbal support we can give a survivor break down into three categories: affirming, countering, and reframing.

....

38   Creative Interventions, "Creative Interventions Toolkit : A Practical Guide to Stop Interpersonal Violence," http://www.creative-interventions.org/tools/toolkit/

AFFIRMING

Affirming means validating a survivor's feelings and experience without catastrophizing. Most of the time, we do a fine job of this nonverbally by unconsciously mirroring the other person's expressions, nodding along, and keeping an open posture, like leaning toward the other person, instead of away from them. But during disclosure, it can be helpful to emphasize affirmation by saying things like, "Wow, that's really not okay" and "I'm so sorry this happened."

COUNTERING

You're bound to run into all kinds of feelings in a survivor as they share what they went through, especially if they're just beginning to process what happened (which, by the way, can happen years after the event, as some survivors need a lot of distance from a situation to feel safe enough to process it). During Shift, you want to gently counter feelings that could lead to isolation or otherwise prevent connection, such as guilt, shame, and self-blame.

Guilt and Self-Blame

I cannot stress enough how much guilt and self-blame undermine our ability to connect with others. When we feel like we are or might be the reason that something bad happened, we're less likely to seek out others, or stay connected when we do. Isolation is dangerous for social mammals, so we need to counter these ideas when talking to survivors.

Even if, in telling you what happened, the survivor names a behavior or choice that you disapprove of or wish they would change, you cannot get hung up on it. You don't have to pretend that you're okay with the behavior or choice. Just gently lead them back to what should be the focus: that they don't deserve the harm that happened to them. You can do this by saying something like, "Yes, maybe taking additional measures if one is walking home after dark is a good idea, but no one deserves to get hurt if they aren't able to arrange a buddy every time. What happened to you is wrong."

There may come a time when you can help a survivor examine things like their choices in partners and other life decisions, but now is not that time. Think about it this way: if a plane's engine fails, do you land the plane, or deliver a monologue about your lack of faith in the operational performance standards for engines? Land that plane!

Some survivors have belief systems or belong to cultures and religions that reinforce ideas that cause guilt and self-blame. If a survivor brings up these ideas, it can be tricky to strike the right balance between respect and countering, both for those who share a survivor's values and beliefs, and for those who don't and therefore have no idea what to say. If you *do* share a survivor's values and beliefs or are well-versed in them, refocus the conversation on something within that belief or value system that is reassuring or help-ful. If you don't, tell the survivor that you hear them and you also know they're someone who lives as much as possible in integrity with their values. Reiterate that everyone is deserving of safety and compassion.

If a survivor brings up that their faith or culture is not very supportive in situations of harm, try to minimize your feedback if you don't share their beliefs or values. Keep an eye on their response! If you get the sense that your words rubbed them the wrong way, apologize and move the conversation along. The apology doesn't have to be elaborate—something like, "That's not helpful, I'm sorry," works fine. Our beliefs and values are deeply entwined with identity, and it's easy for a comment about them to register like a personal attack, especially when someone is activated. Tread with care.

Shift is not a good time to bring up what you think about a survivor's faith or personal beliefs—or their lack of them. It's also probably not the time to encourage them to join your church, temple, meditation practice, coven, or other spiritual group. If you have a faith or belief system that includes something you think might be helpful, you can try sharing it, but keep it brief. Recognize that this suggestion may be off-putting to survivors who don't share your beliefs or are not in the mental headspace to engage on that level. A good way to initiate sharing is to gently test the waters before going all out. For example, rather than inviting them to pray with you then and there, you might ask, "Would you mind if, later, when I pray for safety and healing, I keep you in mind?" Likewise, rather than handing them a bag full of ingredients and a set of complex instructions for a ritual, you might instead offer, "In my practice, we believe that crystals have unseen properties. The one on the table is for protection. You can take it home with you if you feel it will be useful."

Remember that some people have complex histories with faith, so if you get a whiff of resistance, drop it and move along.

Rationalization

Rationalization is another face of self-blame. Survivors have a deep need to take back control as they begin to process what happened and, lacking other options, sometimes the most accessible way to feel in control is to take on some of the blame. The logic goes like this: if the survivor caused the bad thing to happen, then they hold the power to make sure the bad thing never happens again. It is an extremely high-cost strategy due to its ability to isolate a survivor from others, but it's not uncommon. Taking on blame also makes it easier to bear relationships where harm is ongoing.

It can be really hard to hear a survivor rationalize the harm they experienced. Stay calm and be gentle in conveying that nothing makes harm okay.

Protectiveness

You don't need to convince a survivor that the person who harmed them is bad or evil to affirm that what the survivor experienced was harm. In fact, it's preferable to keep any negative feelings about the person who harmed them to yourself. The closer a survivor is to the person who harmed them, the bigger the impulse the survivor may feel to protect them. This reaction can get in the way of a survivor's ability to be in their feelings or cause them to disconnect from you and begin self-isolating.

Harm that happens between people who know each other injures their bond, but it doesn't always sever it. You will encounter survivors who still deeply love the person who harmed them. This stuff is complex, and we make it easier when we remind a survivor it's okay to care about the person who harmed them. The safer we make it for a survivor to feel their feelings, the easier it is for them to begin integrating their experience. Allow the feelings to happen as the survivor makes their way from one end of the emotional spectrum to the other and back again. Tell them you understand why they would feel the way they do, and don't be surprised if the feelings reverse within the course of even a single conversation. Humans are complex! Harm brings up all kinds of stuff! Processing takes time!

Also keep in mind that whether or not a survivor should leave a situation where harm is happening is a complex calibration best left to Shape, when the survivor has more capacity to make choices. Let them know they don't have to make a decision right now, and that you support them no matter what they decide.

As the survivor explores the possibility of leaving the situation where harm is happening, they may experience a lot of indecision. This is not uncommon, and it calls on those of us supporting them to be patient and manage our own feelings. In general, any decision made before a survivor reaches stability should be regarded as tentative—and even then! Life changes are complex, so the vibe we want to put out is: "I support you no matter what you end up deciding to do!"

Absolutism

Many of us don't grow up with stories that offer a lot of nuance. As a result, we see the people in our lives like the characters in those stories: either good or evil. This either-or reasoning can really mess with our heads when we experience harm! If someone harmed us, does that mean they're evil? If they are always doing good for others—and therefore can't be considered evil—are they not capable of harm? Does that mean the harm isn't harm?

These questions are impossible to navigate without nuance, and shifting may call on us to gently introduce it by reminding a survivor that people contain multitudes. We are equally capable of good and ill, and it's not only possible but common for someone to make positive contributions to the lives of others and also do harm.

Minimizing

If a survivor starts to minimize what happened by saying the harm was not a big deal and they can take it, it's possible that they're feeling self-conscious about being so vulnerable. You can soothe that concern by letting them know you think they're resilient. If you get the sense that they're worried about looking cowardly, pathetic or sensitive for having feelings about what happened, remind them that having feelings is like having skin: pain tells us that something is wrong. It is adaptive to feel it and healthy to acknowledge it.

You may also have to do some countering if a survivor begins minimizing in the opposite direction, such as by bringing up people who have it worse. If that happens, acknowledge those other struggles, and remind the survivor that the existence of other harms or large-scale problems doesn't diminish the impact of harm in their life.

A survivor may also minimize by listing all their blessings and privileges. If this happens, let the survivor run through their list. Positive things in our lives (both present and past) are resources that we can think of to make ourselves feel better when we're in a tough place. Sometimes efforts to regulate ourselves by calling on things that bring us joy go a little awry, and instead of feeling better, we end up feeling like we have no right to feel hurt because everything else in our lives is so great. You can help a survivor make sure this doesn't happen when they count their blessings by remind-ing them that having things that bring them joy doesn't mean they can't get hurt, nor are they being ungrateful by feeling hurt.

Take note of the blessings that come up during the conversation (or think back to find some). Resources like blessings or memories the survivor has of fun times with you can be used to derail an encroaching flashback or interrupt an escalating state of activation.

Interrupting is a dicey maneuver when you are trying to stay connected with someone in distress, but you can mitigate the risk of disconnection by telling the survivor what you are trying to do. For example, you might say, "I worry that if we go into more detail about what happened right now you might get into flashback territory, so can we take a break for a second? Maybe take a mental detour and think about the time we ..."

REFRAMING

Hindsight is 20/20 and very helpful for keeping us safe in future situations but, just like counting our blessings, sometimes we can get stuck on what we didn't do or should have done and feel awful about ourselves. If you notice this happening, remind the survivor that their body's response to the harm involved a lot of different things, including cues their body picked up that they aren't conscious of and may never know! From there, you can refocus the discussion from what they should have done to what they did. What they did helped them get out of that situation so they could arrive at this moment, and that is no small thing.

What to Avoid

If not knowing what to say is something you struggle with, you're not the only one. What to say is not part of the body's built-in safety cues toolbox, and as a result, that's where many of us have the most trouble. The aphorism "the road to hell is paved with good intentions" is applicable here. We get nervous, we overthink and then freeze and say nothing, or we don't think at all and say things poorly.

Before we go over some common mistakes, I want you to take a breath and remember that messing up is a shared human experience. We all have moments when we don't know what to say, and moments where we say the wrong thing. Our mistakes can hurt others, but they are rarely irreparable. I refer to my mistakes as my goslings both to make them less frightening and to remind myself that they need tending to. Tending to our mistakes means recognizing we did wrong and owning the impact of our actions. Often, the act of owning our harm is all it takes to begin repair with the person we hurt.

INTERROGATING

Some people think that asking a lot of questions is a good way to show we're engaged and actively listening. This isn't wrong, but some survivors may feel overwhelmed by too many questions, or even interrogated. It's also important to remember that sometimes a survivor discloses harm before they have the language to fully describe what happened. Some harms are complex in that we know something that happened was not okay, but we don't know how to explain it or how to connect the dots to help others see the harm. Then there's the way trauma messes with memory.[39] Sometimes

....

39   van der Kolk, *The Body Keeps the Score.*

we don't remember anything, like the file just didn't save. Other times, it's like we broke the experience into pieces and saved them in several encrypted drives, but can only remember some of the passwords some of the time. This is why accounts of what happened can be so surreal, make so little sense, or feel incomplete. A survivor may remember with uncanny precision every single smell or color they encountered during an experience, for example, but feel lost when it comes to the order of events. This doesn't mean they're lying. You can help them by saying you can see that something bad happened, and they don't have to tell you all the details perfectly for you to believe that something bad happened.

Remember that you're not the police or a district attorney—you are there to support them, and to do that, you don't need all (or any, honestly) of the details. I don't mean you shouldn't ask any questions, but be mindful of how they land and be quick to reassure the survivor if they appear taken aback or put off. A question that to you establishes context—such as "Did you arrange to meet at the bar?"—could feel to the survivor like you're holding judgment, too! Being judged is a common fear and, unfortunately, also a common experience for survivors, so if you start feeling defensive about a survivor's reaction to your attempt to engage with questions, remind yourself that they could be reacting to a fear or prior experience. Reiterate that nothing they did or didn't do makes what happened to them okay, and that the only person responsible for the harm is the one who did the harm.

BLAMING

As you hear what a survivor experienced, you may find your-self uncomfortably gravitating in the direction of blame. I don't think you're a monster. I honestly believe that, most often, blame is driven by a desperate need to make sense out of something terrifying. In blaming, we manufacture a causal effect that makes something scary feel manageable: the bad thing happened *because* the survivor did or didn't do something. We know what the something is, so *the bad thing will not happen to us.* And if the survivor listens to us, it will not happen to them again, either. Problem solved!

It's a clever hack, but the cost to the survivor is too high. We must be brave. Survivors disclose to us in trust and if we mismanage our emotional reaction and blame them, it can have disastrous consequences for them. Experiencing blame from someone they trust has a chilling effect on their ability to connect with others, which magnifies isolation and compounds the harm.

Another way we arrive at blame is when we try to "fix" the situation. Remember that you're not there to tell the survivor what to do or what they should have done differ-ently, but to hold space for their feelings. Assessing and forecasting risk have a place in survivor support, but they are not a part of Shift.

Blame severs the connection between a trusted person and a survivor, sometimes very violently, which can be traumatic in itself. Preliminary research by Cornell

University in conjunction with the anti-harassment group Hollaback! found that the failure of bystanders to respond to harm magnifies the negative impact of harm on a survivor.[40]

Survivors don't need anyone to tell them what they did wrong. I guarantee that no one's a harsher or more thorough judge of everything they could have done better than the survivor themselves. Most survivors will have examined each and every second of what they remember with the precision of a surgeon, berating themselves at every turn for everything they did and didn't do. Trust me when I say that survivors don't need extra help assigning blame to themselves. What they need is another human to meet them in their distress.

If you start to feel the impulse to blame, please consider that you might be scared or having some other unwelcome feeling. It's not unusual to get activated just by hearing an account of harm. Unwelcome feelings like fear can make us react by pushing away the person we think is the cause. Blame disconnects: just as self-blame makes a survivor disconnect themselves from others, we can use blame to disconnect others from us. If you notice yourself wanting to blame, consider telling the survivor that you're scared or

40   Beth A. Livingston, KC Wagner, Sarah T. Diaz, and Angela Lu, "The Experience of Being Targets of Street Harassment in NYC: Preliminary Findings from a Qualitative Study of a Sample of 223 Voices who Hollaback!" The Worker Institute at Cornell Equity at Work Report, 2012, https://www.ihollaback.org/wp-content/uploads/2012/06/corrected-dataILR_Report_TARGET_1B_10232012-1.pdf

having some other intense response. You want to be there for them, but you simply don't have the internal resources to do that in a way that is safe for them and for you. You might ask if there's something else you can do together other than talking to maintain the connection. I firmly believe that we have a responsibility to show up for one another when harm happens, but I also think that it's possible to do this in a way that is responsive to our bodies. Remember: processing is only one way to support a survivor.

Some of us may be called on to show up for a survivor whose actions or choices we don't like. It may tempting to use their regret as an opportunity to push them to change. Remember that now is not the time. This doesn't mean you have to pretend that you approve— it's possible to disapprove *and* counter their self-blame. You might do this by saying something like, "Yes, getting very drunk is not good and you should examine the role of alcohol in your life. But that's a separate thing and doesn't mean you deserved the harm."

REACTING

Activation changes us. When we are activated, our body becomes focused on keeping us safe, which can shut down our social engagement system. This is true for survivors, too. Being activated means a survivor's ability to think about your needs, take care with their words, and access the empathy they're otherwise capable of are temporarily suspended. Shifting resolves this, but while a survivor remains activated, things might get rocky.

It's okay to feel negative feelings toward a survivor if they say something that's hurtful, unexamined, or just annoying. It's also not unheard of to have abandonment issues bubble up when we learn we're among the last people they told or that they didn't know if they could trust us to tell. It is okay to feel the things we feel. What's not okay is reacting to them without thinking.

Because we're not taught to pay attention to our feelings or manage them, sometimes we don't realize we're having feelings until *after* we've reacted to them. Holding space for someone calls on us to be attentive to ourselves so we don't simply react. I include more tips about managing feelings in Chapter 5, but checking in with yourself while engaging with a survivor is a great hack to use in the meantime. Ask yourself: *What do I feel in my body right now? Am I getting activated? Do I need to take a break?*

Talking about harm can be extremely activating. This is especially true if you have experienced a similar kind of harm. Being mindful of our state can help us notice that something's coming up for us so that we can respond with care. It's better to ask the survivor if you can pause the conversation for a bit—or even tell them that you've hit a limit and need to stop talking about harm for the evening—than to try to push through. There is nothing good for us or the survivor on the other side of our limits. It's hard to tell a survivor we're not able to give them the kind of support we think they need, but paying attention to our limits is a crucial skill that will save us a lot of grief (more about that in Chapter 5). When we haven't utterly exhausted ourselves, we're much better able to gently set limits and offer alternative activities that allow us to continue to be present with the survivor while taking care of ourselves.

If the source of your activation is something the survivor said or did that hurt you, please consider waiting until the survivor is no longer in such a vulnerable and reactive place to address it.

If a part of you is upset that the survivor is not being grateful that you're helping them, ask yourself why you require that and whether that's fair. Ideally, you're stepping up because you want to confront harm in your communities, not as a way to feel important or valued. If your self-esteem depends on receiving a "correct" amount of gratitude from those you help, you might want to take a time-out and reflect on your sense of worthiness.

Anger toward the person who harmed is another feeling that can sneak up on us if we're not mindful. It can be challenging to stay calm when we learn a friend was harmed! Again, I'm not saying we're not allowed to have feelings or that we need to hide them from the survivor—it's natural to have feelings! When our feelings reflect what the survivor is feeling, it can even be deeply affirming to them. The problem arises when we can't manage our reactions, like when we're mobilized into aggression toward the person who harmed.

Threatening violence could be triggering to some survivors, or could suck them into a guilt spiral for "betraying" the person who harmed them. We don't want someone who's already running low on internal resources to have to shift *us* back toward calm. Survivors come to us for support, not to do emotional labor for us. Basically, this work is going to make you unlock emotional management on the skill tree and level up like there's no cap.

In my experience, what survivors want most is for their hurt to be witnessed by those they confide in, and acknowledged by the person who harmed. The need for revenge is not an automatic consequence of harm, but something more commonly born in the depths of isolation, disregard, disbelief, and grief. We play a part in ending the feedback loop of harm when we show up to support survivors. We don't need to throw on a cape or jump on our trusty steeds: all we need to do is listen to the survivor, help them shift out of activation, and give them room to be an agent in determining the next steps.

CHEERING UP

When the people around us are able to meet us in our grief, we feel understood and seen. This connection is vital to safety. Unfortunately, the opposite is also true: if we come to someone with grief and they begin joking and trying to cheer us up, our bodies may register that emotional mismatch as a threat. Remember that our neuroception bases assessments about our safety on the emotional states of those around us. Our bodies recognize being surrounded by other humans whose emotional state does not match ours as potentially dangerous. We may not be alone, but we're definitely disconnected. We may even be a target (cue any number of coming-of-age films, from *Back to the Future* to *Mean Girls*). That said, everyone is different. If you know the survivor and think they might respond well to a little humor as the conversation progresses, give it a shot. Just be attentive to their reaction and quick to apologize if it doesn't have the effect you were hoping for.

DISEMPOWERING

When someone shares their experience of harm, some of us feel a strong inclination to want to "fix" things. You might catch yourself telling them what you would have done, for example. Sharing like this is not inherently wrong—we can learn a lot from one another by sharing what we have done or would do in certain situations. However, because of the isolating nature of feelings like self-blame and guilt, it's important to hold back on this until a survivor is ready for Shape. As long as you remain in Shift, your task is giving as many safety cues as you can, listening, validating, and countering feelings that isolate.

A lot of survivors find it helpful to hear how what they *did* do allowed them to survive. This is especially true of survivors who didn't experience a fight or flight reaction to harm. Many of us grew up with a model of survival response that didn't include the freezes, or the much-more-recently acknowledged fawn, which uses cooperation to minimize further harm. Responding to harm by mentally checking out or by being obliging to the person who harmed them can make survivors feel extremely complicit. This is why it's important to affirm survivors, reminding them that our bodies do the best they can with what resources they've got available. Our body's job is to keep us alive, and that doesn't look the same from one body to the next or even from one situation to the next. Sometimes that means fighting, sometimes it means fleeing, sometimes that means being still until it's safe enough to flee, and sometimes it means cooperating. Remind the survivor that they made it, their body did what it had to in order to bring them to this moment, and that's amazing.

Another way we sometimes disempower survivors when trying to help is by telling them what they need to do. Harm fundamentally undermines a survivor's sense of agency and bodily autonomy, so it's important that we not do the same. Our support should reinforce both, rather than further undermining them. We do this by offering a survivor options and letting them decide what happens next, rather than pushing them toward our preferred course of action.

If you catch yourself telling the survivor what they need to do, stop, smile, take a breath and remind yourself what *you* need to do: listen to the survivor, witness their feelings, and validate their survival response.

Calling the police is the first and only thing many people know about responding to harm. I fundamentally believe that if people knew how dehumanizing, disempowering, and even cruel the criminal justice system can be to some survivors of harm, they would approach that option with a great deal more caution. The focus should be on identifying ways to mitigate risks for a survivor who wants to report, rather than trying to convince them that everything will be resolved by calling 911, or, worse, that they have a moral responsibility to do so. When we say things like, "You can prevent this from happening to someone else by being brave enough to report it," we inadvertently prioritize theoretical others over a flesh-and-blood survivor's felt sense of safety.

It's not wrong to want to keep others safe, but it's important to keep priority levels in mind, too. Shift comes first. Once the survivor's nervous system has stabilized, they are better positioned to make decisions about wider community safety, whether that means calling the cops or calling for accountability.

DISMISSING

It's natural to want to make someone who's hurting feel better. Unfortunately, we sometimes attempt this by trying to convince a survivor that what happened was a misunderstanding or not as big a deal as it seems. I call this strategy "arguing with the body." It was the survivor's body that registered the danger cues leading up to and during the experience—hundreds of thousands of them, more than we may ever know or develop language for. Their body took in these cues and determined that the danger was credible and imminent. Don't argue with it. That's not what it needs.

If what the survivor describes sounds to you like an accident or misunderstanding, or not really that big a deal, remind yourself that you don't have the whole picture. You were not there. But also: it doesn't matter. Shift is not about building a legal case. It's about connecting. If you're trying to convince someone that what they feel in their body is not real, *you are not connecting.*

Intent matters, but not here

The intention of the person who caused harm is not a part of Shift, but that's not to say that it doesn't matter. For example, understanding intent *may* help a survivor decide the course of action they want to take. And, as the accountability auditor Michón Neal teaches,[41] intent definitely matters and is a big part of the process for the person who harmed. To begin the work of becoming accountable, the person who harmed will need to do an inventory of their actions and intentions, examine whether their behavior is part of a pattern, and outline a plan to effect the changes needed to make sure they don't harm again.

---

41   Michón Neal, "The Metanoic Portal," https://the-metanoiac-portal. mn.co/

Affirming a survivor's bodily experience of terror can be hard to do when you know the person who harmed. You might find it difficult to imagine that a friend, colleague, mentor, or respected member of a community could cause harm or do anything that would elicit such a visceral terror response in another person. Remember that you don't need to form an opinion right this minute. Right now, there's a person in front of you who has been hurt. They are your focus. Whether the harm was intentional or accidental, whether it was due to carelessness or retaliation, whether it is part of a larger pattern or appears to be a one-off—that doesn't matter right now. Think about it this way: when a friend tells you someone rear-ended their car, do you try to convince them the accident was not intentional, or do you immediately focus on their physical and emotional health by saying, "Oh no! Are you okay?"

The impulse to try to smooth things over by attributing the best intentions to the person who harmed, and convincing the survivor that they misunderstood the situation, is not uncommon. It's another face of fawn, or the cooperative survival response. Members of a species with a biological imperative to connect don't usually seek out conflict within their group. Smoothing things over under different circumstances helps us maintain group harmony and cohesion. But in the case of harm, the price we pay for cooperation is too high. As studies continue to show, many (perhaps most) instances of harm are not one-offs, but part of larger patterns involving multiple types of harm,[42] meaning that by cooperating, we ensure harm continues. Because of how harm causes activation and isolation, this not only impacts those who are harmed, but ripples across the entire social fabric of a group. Without regulation, the activation in a survivor's body can become chronic, making it difficult for them to connect with others, regulate themselves, and help others regulate. As the pattern of harm continues to impact community members, locking more people into chronic activation, the group's overall resiliency goes down and ties begin to fray. Eventually, other nervous systems in the community begin to register that something is wrong. Neuroception isn't conscious—the danger our bodies detect becomes a nameless, abstract unease that eats up our resources and corrodes overall trust and belonging.

Smoothing things over can be a healthy response in many situations, but harm is not one. People who harm create an autonomic ripple effect that undermines the health of entire communities.

MINIMIZING

Gratitude is a powerful force, and sometimes in an effort to help a survivor tap into it, we make the mistake of comparing their experience to something else—often something huge, so their own experience feels less overwhelming. What we

....

42   D. Lisak and P.M. Miller. "Repeat Rape and Multiple Offending Among Undetected Rapists," *Violence and Victims* 17(1), 2002: 73-84. doi: 10.1891/vivi.17.1.73.33638

want is to give them perspective, to tell them that it could be worse and they're blessed it wasn't. Sadly, that's often not the result. Instead of gratitude, what survivors take away from that exchange is a feeling of not being witnessed in their pain.

As I said previously, gratitude is a powerful force and one that plays a role in a survivor's journey to integration, but that force is for them to tap into themselves and not before they've processed what happened. As much as we love them, we cannot fast-forward a survivor to a different part of their inner journey. They have to set out on that path and make the journey on their own.

OVERSHARING

Taking someone into our confidence is a vulnerable act, and it can be destabilizing for a survivor to hear you share thoughtlessly about others. Don't get me wrong: the impulse to connect survivors to one another isn't incorrect. It *is* helpful to know we're not alone in our experiences. But trust matters. A survivor needs the safety of trust to regulate, and that trust is undermined when we act in ways that show we're not mindful of others' consent. We must be trustworthy. Accounts of harm are the experiences of real people, stories that they shared with us in trust. When we're not careful with a survivor's trust, we sabotage the safety they need to regulate.

PUSHING

If the conversation dead-ends, don't push it. Instead, check in about some of the immediate logistics, such as whether a survivor has eaten anything, needs a place to stay, or wants someone to remain with them. These considerations may prompt more conversation about what happened, or about the survivor's fears and worries, or they may naturally segue into a discussion about calling on others to help.

It is normal for a survivor to feel resistant about letting others know what happened to them. Shame, guilt, fear of rejection, and even concern for the person who harmed are not easy obstacles to overcome without a lot of trust. Let a survivor know that they don't have to tell others what happened in order to ask them to show up. As Chapter 3 will show you, there's a lot to being there for a survivor besides processing about the harm!

When You Mess Up

Just so you know, you're going to mess up. You're going to say the wrong thing, you're going to do the wrong thing, you're going to assume the wrong thing. There is no shortage of wrongs you'll do. That's just how it goes. It's okay not to be perfect. The cost of waiting to achieve perfection is too high—survivors can't wait in isolation until we become black belts in nurturance. We have to step up now, do the best we can, and be willing to listen when we make a mistake so we can learn.

If something doesn't land well or things get awkward, acknowledge it. You might say, "Boy, did I make this awkward!" If you say or start to say something that comes across as shaming or comes out wrong, don't even try to explain what you meant. Just stop and say, "Whoa! Did I really just say that? Sounds like I might benefit from some serious self-examination. I'm sorry. That was really messed up!" Then reiterate that no one deserves to experience harm and you want to help.

If you don't notice that you're saying something blaming or hurtful and a survivor calls you out about it, don't argue! Your mission here is to witness the experience of the survivor. That includes listening when they tell you they don't like something you did or said. Don't fight back. Don't argue. Don't explain. Try to understand that the survivor is not only reacting to you, but also to revisiting their experience of harm.

If a survivor is very reactive, they might say things to you rudely or aggressively. Activation impacts language processing and our ability to think linearly, and sometimes the only words within reach for a triggered survivor are the four-letter ones. Just the same: a couple of the most important lessons in my life have been delivered to me by survivors speaking their truth in reactive moments. So don't dismiss what they're sharing based on their tone!

A useful way to respond in this situation is to say, "Thank you for telling me. I'm so sorry I hurt you. I don't want to hurt you." You might repeat that you don't want to hurt them if they say nothing more, and add that you care about them, that you are here for them, that you appreciate them letting you know how to be a better friend and create a safer space for them.

When things go off the rails like this, it's helpful to go back to thinking about safety cues. You can offer tea, water, food, or a blanket, then venture back into dialogue by saying something like, "Thank you for trusting me enough to share what happened. This is really hard and even though I don't know what I'm doing (and you can totally tell!), I am really glad to be here for you." If there is no response, you can ask if the survivor wants to take a break from the conversation and do something else together.

Chapter 3: Shelter

I'm not an extrovert and initially, I was *really* resistant to the idea of bringing in others to help with support work. Growing up nerdy and weird, I didn't have a lot of favorable formative experiences with groups of humans, and so I didn't recognize the importance of involving others in survivor support, either. I managed, but only by chance: the first survivors that I supported needed minimal help stabilizing. They had processed the bulk of their experiences, were not in communities with those who had harmed them, and did not feel inclined to take further action beyond what they each had already done. I won't say it was easy, but it was something that I was able to handle on my own.

Then came one of those tests life throws at you to help you check your answers. In my case, this was an active and ongoing situation in one of my communities that involved multiple survivors, at least two of whom were only just beginning to process what had happened.

Though the survivors worked hard to shift one another, the shifts never lasted long and the activation began to corrode the bonds between them. Siloed in my support role, I couldn't keep up and started to slide into activation myself. As weeks turned to months, I began to regard the survivors I was supporting as one might plutonium cores: unstable, difficult to handle, and eternally in need of management. The more activated I became, the less I was able to help them shift, which only reinforced my view that I was trapped in a criticality accident waiting to happen. I have no doubt that their bodies sensed the autonomic change in me and that this contributed to their own activation—the safety cues were gone. It took me some time to recognize the way I had contributed to the situation—as I mentioned in the Introduction, I have made many errors in this work and this one in particular is among the most humbling. But it is also the most life-changing: I could not both believe that survivors are resilient agents in their lives *and* also lumps of radioactive metal. If support work was making me feel like I was daily toiling at Los Alamos tickling the dragon's tail,[43] then *I* was the one who was doing it wrong. But how could I do it right?

The answer would turn out to be deceptively simple. To quote *The Legend of Zelda*:[44] "It's dangerous to go alone!"

....

43   During World War II, the U.S. government put a bunch of physicists to work at a nuclear weapons facility in Los Alamos, New Mexico. The work involved, among other things, extremely dangerous hands-on experiments to better understand the behavior of plutonium on the brink of nuclear reaction. Aware that one wrong move could result in a fatal radiation dose, the scientists referred to the experiments as "tickling the dragon's tail."

44   *The Legend of Zelda* is a 1986 fantasy action-adventure video game created by Shigeru Miyamoto and Takashi Tezuka. Early in the game, the player encounters an elderly man who provides a sword, saying, "It's dangerous to go alone! Take this." The expression has long since enjoyed a life of its own among nerds and, thanks to the internet, continues to spread and spark joy.

Take this. Copyright: Beautiful Critters, 2017

The Pod

The word *pod* is well-known as the collective noun for whales, seals, and dolphins, but in transformative justice circles, it also refers to any group of people organized in the midst or aftermath of harm to provide support. A pod can be formed for a survivor—to help them stabilize both internally and in their lives—and one can also be convened to help a person who harmed recognize their harm and its impact (something I discuss more in Chapter 6).

"We needed a term to describe the kind of relationship between people who would turn to each other for support," writes Mia Mingus, a core member of the Bay Area

Transformative Justice Collective, which introduced the term in 2016.[45] "These would be the people in our lives that we would call on to support us with things such as our immediate and ongoing safety, accountability and transformation of behaviors, or individual and collective healing and resiliency."

Though the idea of calling people together for support after harm may feel very new to some of us, doing so is a well-established response to harm and stress among social mammals. As I mentioned in the discussion about the many things our bodies do to survive, social mammals have a sophisticated, cooperative response to harm. Dubbed the "*tend and befriend*" response in the academic literature, and fawn among survivors, this coming together and cooperating by humans in cases of stress or threat is increasingly recognized to be on equal footing with fight and flight.[46] Humans have been seeking protection and shelter in groups for a very long time, and pods are one way to tap into it for safety-building.

Whether or not a survivor decides to take action to address the harm, and whether or not a survivor needs help with everyday tasks, surrounding them with a group of people whose focus is their well-being is one of the most

45   Bay Area Transformative Justice Collective, "Pods and Pod Mapping Worksheet," 2016. https://batjc.wordpress.com/pods-and-pod-mapping-worksheet/
46   Shelley E. Taylor, "Tend and Befriend: Behavioral Bases of Affiliation under Stress," *Current Directions in Psychological Science* 15, 6 (Dec. 2006): 273–277, https://wesfiles.wesleyan.edu/courses/PSYC-317-jwellman/Week%207%20-%20Oxytocin/Taylor%202006.pdf

effective means of recalibrating a survivor's sense of safety. A group generates more safety cues than a single person ever will. Connection with a single person is powerful—as Stephen W. Porges says, humans have a biological imperative to connect[47]—but connection with a group is *belonging*. It is in belonging that we feel sheltered, and being sheltered has the power to heal.[48]

FIRE SEASON

The autonomic nervous system is incredibly responsive, which means that no shift is permanent. Even if you help a survivor regulate masterfully after a spike, there will be others. This is especially true when the survivor is first beginning to process the harm, or is part of a community or industry alongside the person who harmed them. In some scenarios, regulating a survivor is like California during fire season: no sooner have you put out a fire in Malibu than you have another one starting a little farther north in Calabasas, or inland in San Bernardino, or south in Oceanside, or very far north in the mountains accessible only to parachuting smokejumpers. You wouldn't expect one fire engine to be enough during a red flag warning, and neither can one person alone do the work of shifting during times of high activation. Here in California, we get backup from other states

47   Porges, *The Pocket Guide to the Polyvagal Theory*.
48   Taylor, "Tend and Befriend."

all the time—in 2018, seventeen different states[49] showed up, as well as at least two crews from other countries.[50] I'm not trying to tell you to be like California, just to remember that we do better together.

While I don't think it's *impossible* to support a survivor without help and, in some situations, safety concerns might leave few other options, I do want to warn you that it's difficult. Being on call to help someone regulate so frequently requires a level of internal resources most people simply don't have. This kind of work is hard even for professionals who have the tools and training to do it. So please, if things are not so dangerous that you have no other options, do not try to support a survivor on your own.

The single most important thing that we can do to be effective in survivor support is to take care of ourselves, and calling on others goes a long way to doing that. I talk more about other forms of self-care in Chapter 5, but for now I will remind you of my nuclear gosling: if we get activated, we stop being able to help a survivor shift and that, in turn, may *increase* their activation. Getting others involved helps distribute the load, which lets us recharge and provides a survivor with a sense of belonging.

....

49   FireRescue1, "Firefighters from around the U.S. travel to help in Calif. wildfires," November 14, 2018, https://www.firerescue1.com/mutual-aid/articles/392924018-Firefighters-from-around-the-U-S-travel-to-help-in-Calif-wildfires/
50   Kellen Browning, "53 firefighters from Australia and New Zealand arrive in Redding," *The Sacramento Bee*, August 6, 2018, https://www.sacbee.com/latest-news/article216206915.html

BELONGING

When a group rallies around a survivor, that act transmits more safety cues than a single person ever could. These cues signal to a survivor not only that they matter, but that they *belong*. This understanding is transformational on a somatic level: belonging is an anchor to safety, and this anchor is what enables a survivor to start to regulate themselves. The more sheltered they feel, the better a survivor can put out *their own fires*.

The effect holds even when people around a survivor don't know explicitly about the harm—provided they're there for a survivor and their emotions don't clash with those of the survivor. If you've ever been sad around people who are laughing and having fun, you understand what I mean when I talk about emotions this way. It can be jarring and even upsetting to hold grief or feel distressed when the people around us are playing and laughing, even if we know that they're not laughing at us. Remember that our bodies sense being among people whose emotions are different than our own as potentially dangerous, as it could mean rejection from group members or that we find ourselves among people who don't see us as one of their own.

Fostering a sense of belonging does not require a survivor to disclose what they experienced. To be involved, other people need to know just enough to be attentive to the survivor and to keep pace with them emotionally. It can be as simple as telling them that the survivor is going through a tough time and needs support over the next several weeks.

That's it! In my experience, it's actually a lot more common for a survivor to choose to disclose to people *after* they've shown up for pod work.

§

I cannot emphasize enough the healing power of belonging. Often in conversations about harm, I hear about the healing power of talking about what happened, and while I don't disagree that breaking the silence is a powerful part of the journey, I think this analysis is incomplete. Survivors who break the silence and are dismissed or not believed do not find disclosure healing. Even those survivors whose disclosures of harm are met by an avalanche of #ibelieveher and #believesurvivors still might not find relief in breaking the silence. What we are missing is the power of taking emotional shelter among others and feeling like we belong.

Disclosure has the power to bring people together. If receptive people are on the other side of a disclosure, that disclosure will punch through isolation, make contact, and bring a survivor to connection. It matters who is on the other side of disclosure: if a disclosure does not meet a receptive listener and the survivor is rejected or shamed, that can be extremely damaging.

Sometimes the damage survivors experience when they disclose is not intentional. Sometimes bystanders take to heart that survivors need to be believed and so they set about interrogating the survivor to ascertain the guilt of the person who harmed them. This is not good! We've talked about what activation does to the brain, how critical parts

go offline. We need to become more mindful about the
order of priority. When someone we know shows up at our
door bleeding profusely, do we demand that they prove the
guilt of the person who harmed them? Do we require them
to explain themselves before we let them in? Of course not.
We take them in and stop the bleeding.

There is healing in being believed—no question about
it. But if we're not willing to connect with survivors *before*
we ascertain all the details, we do more harm than good.
On the other side of this coin are the bystanders who
think that saying that they believe is sufficient to catalyze
an instantaneous, miraculous healing. It doesn't work like
that. "I believe you" is like disclosure, in a way: it can mark
the beginning of a connection or fade into the vast dark-
ness of isolation. What made Me Too—as it was originally
conceived by Tarana Burke—so powerful was its ability to
catalyze a human connection. The movement's emanation
as a hashtag doesn't entirely fail at facilitating connection,
but its memeification and politicization have changed what
it brings survivors.

I want to be careful not to imply that the internet has
nothing to offer a survivor—Tarana Burke was on Myspace
when she came up with Me Too, after all.[51] The internet has
allowed countless survivors to connect, find the language to
describe what they've been through, begin processing with

51   Linette Lopez and Chris Snyder, "Tarana Burke on why she created
the #MeToo movement – and where it's headed" Business Insider,
December 13, 2017, https://www.businessinsider.com/how-the-metoo-
movement-started-where-its-headed-tarana-burke-time-person-of-year-
women-2017-12

others, and find the validation and courage they need to break out of isolation. The internet is a tool and, as such, it can be used to incredible effect, including forging the connections that shelter us on a bodily level. In addition, I do think hashtags such as #metoo and #ibelieveher and #believesurvivors are a powerful way to signal to survivors in our lives that we're safe for them to approach.

We have a lot of the pieces that we need to support survivors fully. We just need to put them all together.

What a Pod Does

Pod work refers to the things people do to provide support. What "support" means will vary depending on the situation and the survivor. There are a lot of ways to show up for a survivor!

Many survivors will want to talk about what happened to them, and some will want to process at length. Some will immediately find the words they need to begin processing, while others will need help developing the language to describe what happened. Some will feel called to examine what they went through very thoroughly, combing over every detail. Some may do extensive research about some aspect of the experience, read every book and paper they can get their hands on, and then want to discuss what they find. And still others will prefer not to talk about it too much more once they disclose. Harm happens to all kinds of people—and we each have our own way of working through it.

As I've mentioned before, processing is not the only thing people can do to support a survivor. Another area where supporters excel is in the to-do list. No matter what the harm is, there are always things to be done in life—errands to run, groceries to buy, meals to cook, kids to care for, pets to walk, litter boxes to clean, laundry to do. People can take on these tasks as a way to step up without knowing any specifics about the harm, or when they aren't able to do much processing or shifting with a survivor. (It is an unfortunate truth that while other survivors are the most helpful people to process with, they're also the most likely to get triggered and need to take a step back!)

OPERATING WITHIN RISK

Sometimes survivors of ongoing harm cannot leave a situation where harm is happening. Sometimes they don't want to leave. Sometimes making a decision either way takes time and is best dropped to Shape priority level with other big life considerations. That's okay. Supporting a survivor means meeting them where they're at, and sometimes that means operating within ongoing risk.

This kind of support will test you, but you don't have to reinvent the wheel. In 2018, Creative Interventions released an updated edition to their manual for responding to harm, which dedicates an entire section to helping survivors stabilize within situations of ongoing harm. The *Creative Interventions Toolkit* is available online for free and offers the best advice and tools I've seen in this arena. The book is a whopper, but if operating within risk applies to the survivor you're supporting, I strongly recommend you read at least some of Chapter 4B: Staying Safe: How Do We Stay Safe?.

One of the worksheets that I use the most in survivor support is the Creative Interventions Risk Assessment Chart.[52] The chart lays out all risks—direct and indirect—that a survivor is facing or feels concerned about.

Risk, danger, or harm	Who or what is the cause	Target of risk, danger or harm	Who is looking out for safety	What safety action and under what circumstances

The first column is for the risk, danger, or harm that a survivor is worried about—and, again, their answers may not be directly related to the person who harmed them. A survivor could be concerned about becoming homeless if they leave a situation where harm is happening when they don't have the means to lease their own place, for example. The second column specifies who or what is the cause of the risk, danger, or harm. The third column is for who would be impacted if the risk, danger, or harm in the first column actually happened. The next two columns are where the pod steps in. The fourth outlines who among those supporting a survivor will handle logistics to mitigate this risk or respond if it happens, and the fifth lists the actions they'll take. In

52   Creative Interventions, "Creative Interventions Toolkit."

addition, Creative Interventions suggests assigning danger levels to each risk. They use: No risk now, Low, Moderate, High, Emergency, and More information needed. (There is no column for danger levels because these are subject to change any time a chart is reviewed.)

A breakdown of potentialities like this is very important for survivors operating within ongoing harm, but it can also be useful for other situations, such as a survivor who is considering coming forward about the harm they experienced.

ALL THE WAYS OF SHOWING UP

Some survivors will tell you that they're fine and don't need any logistical help, and others will have trouble receiving it even when they could use it. You'll probably have to remind them a couple of times that the purpose of getting others involved is to transmit a many-person message of safety to the survivor's body. You may have to brainstorm different ways people can show up for them that don't feel uncomfortable, such as having friends come over to watch their favorite films or help cook a dinner for everyone to enjoy.

Though safety cues seem to have the most power in person, friends who are not local can participate as well, for instance by sharing a joyful memory they have with the survivor, making a feel-good playlist for them, or making some other kind of personalized gesture. I've asked friends for interesting scientific papers as a way of distracting myself to prevent overwhelm, and I've responded to calls for support requesting videos of pets being cute. Your mileage will vary, even from one day to the next. Get creative—there's something out there that's likely to resonate.

Showing up takes different forms, shapes, and sizes. As you've probably already noticed, some of it takes work, but a lot of aspects can be fun. That's an important thing to recognize and remember: keeping pace with a survivor emotionally does not mean we're not allowed to offer them opportunities to laugh, have fun, and experience joy. In fact, one of the most important things that people providing support can do for a survivor is arrange for the sort of fun things that friends so often do: having a Netflix marathon, hiking, hosting a tabletop game night, learning to throw axes, having a jam session, dancing, doing boxing drills, restoring a classic car, picking wild mushrooms, fishing, planting potatoes, getting a manicure, playing video games, horseback riding—whatever it is that you do that the survivor is or may be into. There are only three rules:

1. Let the survivor choose if they want to participate or not.
2. Don't make them feel guilty for not rallying, changing their mind at the last moment, or bailing in the middle of the activity.
3. Don't stop asking them to hang out (and reminding them that they can say no!).

There's an amazing (if disputed[53]) meme that circulates on social media from time to time featuring a drawing of the

53   Some fans dispute that the quote reflects the relationships in the Hundred Acre Wood. I have not engaged with these stories for many decades and so defer to them on this point. That aside, I still find the message resonant and important.

donkey from Winnie-the-Pooh with the caption, "One awesome thing about Eeyore is that even though he is basically clinically depressed, he still gets invited to participate in adventures and shenanigans with all of his friends and they never expect him to pretend to feel happy, they just love him anyway, and they never leave him behind or ask him to change." I want you to make that your motto.

CONTAINERING

Before I wrap up this conversation about the many ways of showing up, I want to take a moment to mention anger. If experience is any indication, anger is a natural part of the process for many survivors. It makes sense to me: anger is a catalyst and a tool of discernment. As a catalyst, anger helps us get to our feet again. As a tool of discernment, it shows us where a boundary was crossed or where a limit needs to be placed. Anger tells us who has not been safe for us to be ourselves with.

To uncover what our anger can teach us, we must work with it, and to do that constructively, we need support. If our bodies don't feel safe, anger could easily catalyze an aggressive fight response instead of revealing its wisdom to us. Those who give a survivor support need to provide the safety cues that a survivor needs to begin that inner work.

Witnessing and holding space for someone who is experiencing anger can be frightening for some people, and for this reason it's very important for pod members to listen to their bodies and take care of themselves. Policing a survivor's anger (or other feelings for that matter) does not provide them with any safety cues!

It is much better for pod members to work out a way to take turns holding space for a survivor as a designated "anger buddy." (By anger buddy, I mean someone who is willing to witness anger, accord it the respect it deserves, and, most importantly, help a survivor container it so that no one comes to harm while it is being transmuted.)

I recommend taking turns when doing anger containering work because there may be a lot of anger to work through—especially when a survivor carries not only anger about the original harm, but also anger over the feelings of abandonment from coming forward and not being heard or believed. In my experience, the longer it takes for a survivor to reach shelter, the more anger there is and the more unwieldy it is.

If it seems like a survivor's anger is more than you or other pod members can handle, it's important to let the survivor know that this is about you and not them. Be very explicit in letting them know that they're not the problem, that the problem is that you and other pod members can't create the kind of container that will honor and nourish the survivor in their work with anger.

When I talk about "honoring anger," I do not mean giving it free rein to catalyze aggression. It is possible (and advisable) to disapprove of harm while holding space for angry feelings and exploring safe avenues of release for those feelings. I'm partial to pulverizing discarded inanimate objects with baseball bats, but I've heard really good things about throwing axes, smashing pumpkins, and good, old-fashioned knocking down cans with slingshots. The exercise is only limited by your imagination and a survivor's interest (and ethics and lab safety, obviously).

A recent study[54] led by psychologist Lindie Hanyu Liang at Wilfrid Laurier University found that acts of "symbolic retaliation" seem to have a soothing effect, helping a person restore their sense of justice. That study allowed workers to take out frustration against colleagues on dolls, but I bet you can make anything work in a pinch. In the 1990s cult classic *Tales From The Hood*, for example, a little boy crushed the monster who terrorized him by drawing it on paper and crumpling the paper in his hands. A method predating paper was brought to my attention more recently by the Egyptologist Joann Fletcher, who related that a common way of cursing a person in ancient Egypt involved writing their name on a piece of pottery, then smashing it.[55]

Symbolic retaliation could be really fun for some, but if it's not fun for you or the survivor you're supporting, that's okay!

....

54   L.H. Liang et al., "Righting a Wrong: Retaliation on a Voodoo Doll Symbolizing an Abusive Supervisor Restores Justice," *Leadership Quarterly* 29, 4 (August 2018): 443–456, https://doi.org/10.1016/j.leaqua.2018.01.004
55   BBC Two, "Immortal Egypt with Joann Fletcher," Episode 2: Chaos, 2016 (minute 13).

Containering anger is one of those aspects of processing in pod work that can be delegated to a therapist, life coach, emotional alchemist, or some other person who is professionally trained or skilled in emotional stewardship.

Building a Pod

The two most common hurdles to sheltering a survivor are their own fear and worry. It's a vulnerable thing to call on others for help, even when we know that we don't have to disclose what happened.

Some types of ongoing harm may involve control and isolation, preventing a survivor from involving more people in roles of support. Listen to the survivor as you discuss their concerns to get a sense of where the resistance to involving others is coming from. If the harm you're dealing with is ongoing and involves isolation, you will be limited in how you can bring Shelter into being. I provide resources for situations involving ongoing harm in Chapter 4.

WHO YOU GONNA CALL?

The survivor green-lights the idea of a pod, you jump into action, pen in hand or finger on screen, and ... they can't think of anyone. This is a known bug.[56] It's common for survivors

---

56   As in software bug: an error or failure in the code.

to draw a blank when asked who they might call on, and sometimes it takes a little creativity to flesh out a good list. A good hack to get around this hurdle is to ask the survivor questions. The most obvious is whether they've told anyone else about what happened, or if they've thought about doing so. Not everyone that a survivor has told may turn out to be someone who can show up for pod work, but at first, I jot everyone down and put an asterisk next to the name of anyone who's local. Then you can flip the question on its head and ask a survivor whether they've supported anyone who's gone through a similar situation, or some other emotionally intense hardship. This renders a different bunch of people: individuals a survivor has already taken emotional shelter with. This sheltering doesn't necessarily have to be recent—it only needs to involve emotional investment.

Another question you might ask is: Who is dependable? People who are reliable and good at getting things done are fantastic in general and a great blessing in pods, especially in situations with larger logistical moving parts. You know the sort of person—they may not always know what to say, but give them a task that aligns with their skills, and they're on it!

When I first started supporting survivors, I stayed in the reliable cohort by chasing after to-do items and saying things like "Feelings are messy. I don't do messy." Though I often ended up doing a decent amount of shifting *and* processing (being detail-oriented is an incredible skill to offer survivors who are trying to wrap their heads around what happened), I somehow still managed to hold on to the belief that I was not very good at people. It felt true because I'd never learned how to be present with people or hold space for them, and coupled with developmental delays in social skills, I had all the evidence I needed to cling to that belief. It never occurred to me that this stuff is learned, and though missing developmental benchmarks makes that learning harder, it's not like we lose the ability to learn. Learning is lifelong.

Many of us grow up being told that we're socially awkward, we are bad at people, or we are incapable of reading social cues. It's the verb that does it: *are* denotes an immutable state of being, an aspect of one's self that cannot be altered. And none of it is helped by the common misuse of Asperger's as a synonym for sociopath. The discussion of neurodiversity with regard to connection, regulation, and other facets crucial to survivor support is a complex one beyond the scope of this primer, but I wanted to take a moment to tell you that we all have something to contribute to survivor support, and that something is a lot more than we tend to realize. I have done survivor support with other individuals diagnosed or identified on the spectrum, and I know there's room for all of us in this work and that many of us have gifts when it comes to others[57] that are only now being recognized.

I'm going to leave you with something my friend Lea Kissner once said to me that helped me immensely when I was grappling with this challenge myself: "When we don't come equipped with a native human OS[58] and have to build it, sometimes we discover we human better than humans."

Other good list-making questions for a survivor are: Who makes them feel good? Who makes them laugh? Who invites them out to do fun things? People like this are usually not the first ones we think of when we experience a hardship, but we don't need to process or tackle complex life logistics all the time. Sometimes, after a long week of pulling our lives back together, we just want to be able to do something

....

57   "Results showed that adults with ASD [autism spectrum disorder] are unimpaired in processing emotions based on counterfactual reasoning, and in fact showed earlier sensitivity to inconsistencies within relief contexts compared to TD [typically developing] participants. This finding highlights a previously unknown strength in empathy and emotion processing in adults with ASD, which may have been masked in previous research that has typically relied on explicit, response-based measures to record emotional inferences, which are likely to be susceptible to demand characteristics and response biases." Jo Black, Mahsa Barzy, David Williams, and Heather Ferguson, "Intact counterfactual emotion processing in autism spectrum disorder: Evidence from eye-tracking," *Autism Research*, December 21, 2018. https://onlinelibrary.wiley.com/doi/full/10.1002/aur.2056
58   A "native" piece of software is one that is developed for use on a specific platform or device. OS is an abbreviation for operating system.

else, something that has nothing to do with harm. People who are the life of the party are wonderful for this.

Another way to flesh out the list is to ask a survivor to think of people they liked at current and former places of work. (If the harm happened at work, keep in mind that people in some positions are legally required to report harm to human resources, so tread carefully. You don't want to set anything in motion before a survivor is ready.) What about other communities they're part of? Do they have hobbies or activities they enjoy that have a social component?

WITH A LITTLE HELP FROM OUR TECH

Another great hack for list-making is to take a look at phone logs, texts, emails, instant messages, and money-sharing apps. We leak a lot of data with our tech, and a lot of it involves the people who are active in our lives. Invite the survivor to take a look: Do any of them belong in the list?

Social media is a strange beast. Some people have a lot of friends and followers who are not really a part of their lives, and in this case, smaller private-messaging groups and closed communities may be the more useful place to start. Ask the survivor to take a look: Could any of those people be part of a pod?

Other sources of potential pod members are activity feeds and threaded replies, which reveal who a survivor tends to engage with. Frequent engagement doesn't necessarily mean a person is someone the survivor wants in their lives, of course, as adversarial usage of social media shows us every day. But it's still worth asking, and you'd be surprised—sometimes pods end up full of the people we would least expect. "'Pod people' don't fall neatly along traditional lines," says Mia Mingus of the Bay Area Transformative Justice Collective. "The criteria we would use for our pod people is not necessarily the same as what we use (or get taught to use) for our general intimate relationships."

In addition to using frequent contacts to flesh out a list of potential supporters, I've also experimented with more direct opt-in methods. During a crisis, I once posted a status message saying that I was struggling and wanted my friends to check in with me when they had a chance, and then populated my list with the names of those who responded. (To illustrate my earlier point that disclosure is not necessary to get support, I'll tell you the precise percentage of people I eventually told out of those who responded: 1.14 percent. I really mean it when I say that we can do this without requiring a survivor to disclose before they're ready.)

AN ISLAND ENTIRE OF ITSELF

Occasionally, a survivor's list may be very short. Some harms are extremely isolating, and chronic activation can make it tough for a survivor to forge and maintain bonds with others. There are also more mundane reasons for this: we live in a society in which people move all the time, and where it's increasingly difficult to give our social ties the time and energy they deserve. Activation, isolation, and already weak ties combine into a major obstacle to pod-building, but if I have

learned anything in the time I have been doing this work, it is
that our bodies are not particular. In matters of survival they
will make do.[59] It makes sense—we have survived as a species
as long as we have not by going it alone, but by hunkering down
together. The trauma specialist Bessel van der Kolk puts it like
this: "Study after study shows that having a good support network constitutes the single most powerful protection against
becoming traumatized."[60] And I have come to believe that it
is possible for those of us who don't yet have one to borrow it.

The first option, if you happen to live in the same area
as the survivor, is to bring them into *your* support system.
Would the survivor be open to spending some time with
your people? We tend to select for people like ourselves in
our friendships, and if you're up for this kind of work, it's
likely that several of your friends will be as well.

Another option—one that's useful for survivors who are
not nearby—is to encourage them to get online. If there's
one place that the internet shines as a tool, it is in the chasm
of isolation. As #metoo and other hashtags continue to

....

59   Humans will even tend and befriend nonliving things, develop
cooperative relationships with them, and mourn them when they leave
us. See the following examples:
Zaria Gorvett, "How Humans Bond with Robot Colleagues,"
BBC, May 31, 2018, http://www.bbc.com/capital/
story/20180530-how-humans-bond-with-robot-colleagues
Megan Garber, "Funerals for Fallen Robots," *The Atlantic*, September
20, 2013, https://www.theatlantic.com/technology/archive/2013/09/
funerals-for-fallen-robots/279861/
Brent Rose, "The Sad Story of a Real Life R2-D2 Who Saved Countless
Human Lives and Died," Gizmodo, December 28, 2011, https://gizmo-
do.com/the-sad-story-of-a-real-life-r2-d2-who-saved-countless-5870529
60   van der Kolk, *The Body Keeps the Score*

make clear, hundreds of thousands of survivors are online, and many of them are ready to talk about what happened to them and help others process. Networks like Twitter, Facebook, and Instagram let users search for public accounts posting about these topics, which can help a survivor start connecting with others. Facebook in particular has a number of communities designed to facilitate forging such relationships. Tumblr has a surprising number of survivor blogs dedicated to processing and affirming other survivors, Medium hosts several articles about it and enables readers to reach out and connect with authors, and reddit runs several boards for survivors of different types of harm.

My only advice with regard to the internet is to ask a survivor to keep an eye on whether they feel connected in their interactions. Are they talking with people and getting closer, or are they broadcasting into an abyss? It can be affirming to consume a lot of reporting about the latest harm to hit the national news—it can even help a survivor develop the language they need to describe what they experienced— but does doing so help them feel more connected? If using a certain service is causing them to feel activated and not helping them connect with others, encourage them to take a sabbatical from that service and try something new.

Another option is to try warmlines, which are a little like crisis hotlines, except they're non-emergency and tend to be run by peers with lived experience. Unlike many crisis lines, warmlines aim to prevent forced intervention by social services or police, focusing instead on helping people regulate their feelings, feel heard, and even locate local resources like support groups. They're pretty great, and definitely something worth looking up in a survivor's area, whether they think they'll need them or not.

NARROWING DOWN

If brainstorming turns up lots of potential pod members, some narrowing down may be in order. Ask the survivor to go down the list and check in with their bodies about who feels like a "no," who feels like a "maybe," and who feels like a "yes." My ideal pod has at least six people in it, but that is just a personal preference. I've worked in pods with as few as two others and as many as 15. My advice is to shoot for a list of finalists that has a few more people than you think you'll need. Not everyone has the bandwidth to be involved fully or even partially all the time. Some people who are game for it may not be available now, and some who are available now may not be available later.

If you find that narrowing down isn't necessary, for example if most of the survivor's people are not local or your list simply has plenty of room to grow, ask the survivor if they would be open to meeting friends of yours who are awesome like you.

Getting People Involved

How we invite people to show up for pod work depends on the situation and the survivor. As I mentioned earlier, I once posted an update on social media calling on friends to check in on me and then recruited pod members from those who did. The friends-only post said simply, "I'm going to need my friends to check in on me over the next few days. I'm not okay." (I later updated it with clarification, adding that I was not at immediate risk of any harm and making a more specific request about what I needed.)

Much more often, a survivor will choose to privately reach out to each person on the list, or give you the go-ahead to do it for them. Asking can be hard, and you can take a load off the survivor by offering to handle it. A simple way to ask people on someone's behalf is, "Our friend Survivor is going through a really hard time right now and I'm gathering friends to help provide some support over the coming weeks. Some of the things we're hoping people might help with are ... Do you have the bandwidth to join us?"

Recruiting others is not the only part of pod setup that you can help with. I've known survivors who didn't want to disclose to friends, not because they didn't want people in their lives to know what had happened, but because they couldn't face the idea of catching everyone up. They didn't want to deal with questions or find themselves in a situation where they had to take care of other people's feelings about what had happened to them. Once I offered to be the one to do it, to field all questions and get people to understand that the survivor did not want to talk about the harm, the survivor was on board.

You might also want to preemptively sign up to handle anyone who gets a little pushy about learning more details about what happened before the survivor decides to tell them. I've not run into this very often, but it does happen. People who do this aren't trying to be jerks—most of them really want to help!—but like most of us, they were never taught how. While you cannot promise the survivor everyone will know just what to do, you can let them know that you've got them covered when it comes to herding the well-meaning supporters in the right direction.

Pod Mapping

The Bay Area Transformative Justice Collective uses a visual system to map the people available to help support a survivor. Called the Pod Mapping Worksheet, it sketches out individuals, groups, and other resources that are on standby or can be tapped for assistance.

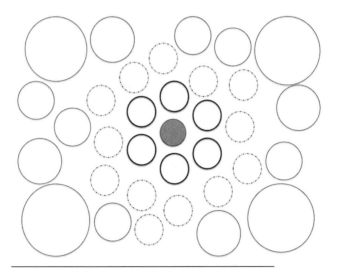

Bay Area Transformative Justice Collective Pod Mapping

The Pod Mapping Worksheet places the survivor in a circle in the center, with pod members in bolded circles like radiating petals around them. Beyond them are circles made of dashed lines, representing folks who'd be great additions to the pod but are not yet fully involved (because they have not yet been asked or they aren't reliably available), though the circles could also be used to denote pod members who don't yet have a strong bond with a survivor. Lastly, the larger circles at the edges of the worksheet represent resources—service organizations, warmlines, support groups, faith groups, a regional transformative justice collective, and so on.

The Pod Mapping Worksheet is flexible, meant to be responsive to the needs of survivors. I've used it as described when a survivor decides to initiate a call for accountability from the person who harmed them, for example. But I've also used it for survivors who had only just disclosed to me. In these cases, the bolded circles represented people who knew specifics about the harm, the dashed circles represented those who were supporting without knowing details about the harm, and the larger outside circles represented service providers or resources to help the survivor stabilize—both within themselves, and in their lives.

I've also used the worksheet to map a survivor's self-care options. I used the bolded circles to highlight people the survivor could tap for processing, talking, or other kinds of one-on-one activity, the dashed circles for independent activities that the survivor found soothing, and the bigger circles for group activities that made them feel good.

Chapter 4: Shape

In shifting and sheltering with a survivor, we make it possible for them to get back to a level of stability that allows them to start making decisions about their life. These decisions—made from a place of safety, greater internal resources, and bandwidth—shape the new chapter of a survivor's life, which gives this part of the process its name: *Shape*.

Survivors in situations where harm is ongoing may get to this point and start to seriously consider making plans to leave. Or they may decide to stay with the help of a community intervention aimed at minimizing further harm. Survivors who are not in contact with the person who harmed them may decide that they want them to witness the impact of their actions and make repair. Or they may want nothing to do with the person who hurt them. Still others may want to make sure that no others come to harm by the person who harmed them—without having to interact with that person further. And yet other survivors may want something else entirely. Shape is about helping a survivor determine what their goals are and the steps they need to take to bring them into being. In this chapter, we'll explore a handful of things within two domains that a survivor may decide to tend to. The first is their personal domain,[61] which involves therapy and other aspects of their recovery or healing journey, as well as decisions about how to proceed when they remain in contact with someone who harmed them. The second domain a survivor may tend to is that of their community, which may involve harm-reduction efforts like callouts and offers of accountability to the person who harmed them. This list is by no means exhaustive.

Tending to the Self

There are many ways for survivors to tend to their personal domains after harm. The culture, tradition, or faith that they're part of may offer an approach toward resolution that serves them well. Other times, they may be called to reach beyond what they know, and come to you for suggestions. This section contains my suggestions, which may or may not be applicable to your situation. I mention therapy specifically here not because I think it's the only valid way to begin the healing journey, but because I came into it with a lot of distrust and was surprised to find it helpful. What worked for me, however, may not work for others. When it comes to a survivor's path, there is no single right answer. Any tool for

....

61   I am in the debt of the consent educator Betty Martin, from whom I learned about the concept of the personal domain.

healing can also hurt in the wrong context, so encourage a survivor to tread lightly and listen to their gut.

THERAPY

One of the primary methods available for survivors looking to tend to themselves is therapy. I wish we learned about different therapeutic modalities as early as we do shapes in geometry. I was in my thirties before I learned that different life struggles call for completely different psychological interventions. I thought all therapy was talk therapy, where maybe if you talked long enough, you would eventually stumble on some kind of truth—or a pill prescription that may or may not help. The idea that I might request to collaborate with a therapist in creating a treatment plan with clear goals and objectives still feels revolutionary to me. Now that I know that it is possible to take this kind of active role in our mental health—and that the correct combination of modalities can not only help a survivor in the aftermath of harm, but equip and empower us in our healing—I strongly encourage other survivors to explore this possibility in their lives if it is at all possible for them to do so.

For many of us in the United States, therapy is often inaccessible due to its cost and, in some cases, discrimination.[62] Even those of who have insurance may be severely

....

62   Heather Kugelmass, "'Sorry, I'm Not Accepting New Patients': An Audit Study of Access to Mental Health Care," *Journal of Health and Social Behavior* 57, no. 2 (2016): 168-183, https://doi. org/10.1177/0022146516647098

constrained in terms of the number of sessions we're able to receive within our plans, as well as the kind of practitioners we may see. (American insurance companies are notorious for not being accurate on their lists of in-network providers, especially when it comes to therapists[63].) This inaccessibility can hurt survivors, since psychology is such a specialized field and not every therapist has the training to help us.

There is no one-size-fits-all approach to trauma: what happened matters, as does whether it happened once or chronically. Equally important is who the survivor is, what coping strategies they have, and how the experience has affected and continues to affect them, among other things.

While a detailed list of available therapies and how they can help a survivor is beyond the scope of this primer, I will offer you some books that have helped me and other survivors I know find our way:

» *The Body Keeps the Score: Brain, Mind, and Body in the Healing of Trauma* by Bessel van der Kolk[64]

....

63   Liz Kowalczyk, "Aetna settles with state over 'ghost networks'," *The Boston Globe*. December 11, 2018, https://www.bostonglobe.com/business/2018/12/11/aetna-settles-with-state-over-ghost-networks/AmnsHaunRlhj50uGqYwaeN/story.html

64   In 2018, van der Kolk was fired from the Trauma Center he founded and called out by peers at the Justice Resource Institute for creating a toxic workplace environment. Van der Kolk sued, and while eventually he dismissed his suit and acknowledged "in times of stress, there is room for me to improve my interpersonal sensitivity," there is no record that he's undertaken any work to manage his responses to activation. His research and books are important, but letting you exercise informed consent means I have a responsibility to mention these facts. Bessel van der Kolk, "Behind the Globe Article," August 12, 2018, http://web.archive.org/web/20181009214208/https://besselvanderkolk.net/behind-the-globe-article.html

» *In An Unspoken Voice: How The Body Releases Trauma and Restores Goodness* by Peter Levine
» *Journey Through Trauma: A Trail Guide to the Five-Phase Cycle of Healing Repeated Trauma* by Gretchen L. Schmelzer

These three books can be groundbreaking for the survivor who is inclined to learn more both about trauma and ways to address it, but I also feel it's important to mention that all three can be triggering due to language, examples, and case studies. If a survivor hasn't thought of anything for a pod to do yet, reading the books to extract what may be useful is a fantastic task item. It's regrettable that survivors have to do this much research just to figure out what kind of help we might need, and I hope that things will change for us soon, but this is where this country's at right now.

Another way a pod can show up for a survivor in this arena is by locating area therapists that have training in the modalities that a survivor thinks sound helpful. A pod may even offer to give therapists a call to check whether they're part of an insurance network, and if they are not, whether they offer a sliding-scale fee structure.

A number of modalities offer certification programs and have websites that enable potential clients to search for practitioners by area. To find them, try searching for the modality and some keywords, such as "EMDR therapist network" or "somatic experiencing therapist."

Once a survivor finds a therapist or practitioner, encourage them to be choosy. It's okay to interview therapists before committing. The Trauma Center at the Justice Resource Institute recommends asking a potential therapist the following questions:

» What is your formal training background?
» What specific training have you had in the area of trauma?
» How many years have you been treating people for trauma?
» How many people have you treated for trauma?
» What is your treatment philosophy, approach, and methods?
» How will we know when we are finished?

Because feeling welcome is such a big part of internal safety, I also encourage survivors to ask prospective therapists whether they have worked with people of their religious background, race, class, gender identity, orientation, relationship configuration, line of work (if they're in a stigmatized industry), etc., and see how they like their answers. Also, if a survivor is in recovery for substance use or another coping mechanism that has become compulsive, I recommend asking the therapist if they are up to speed on the literature and comfortable working with someone who may occasionally need backup in that area, or if they have an established relationship with another practitioner who can step in if necessary.

If a survivor tries out a therapist but leaves the session feeling unsure whether they like the therapist or whether the session was helpful—or if the session or therapist made them feel worse!—it's okay not to continue seeing them. Therapists are human, and like any human, they don't always have the bandwidth or the tools they need to help us in the ways we need to be helped. But unlike other people in a survivor's life who are doing the best they can in showing up for them, therapists are healers trained to take people into ourselves. They *need* to have the tools and the bandwidth to keep a survivor safe through that process. If working with them doesn't feel right to a survivor, it's okay to walk away and keep looking.

I completely agree with the celebrated psychologist Eugene T. Gendlin, who said "The process of actually changing feels good. Effective working on one's problems is not self-torture. [...] It feels like inhaling fresh air after having been in a stuffy room for a long time." Some aspects of the process will get tough, but the initial steps—establishing trust and getting oriented—should not be among them.

SURVIVORS IN CONTACT

Because harm often happens among people who know one another, many survivors remain near—if not in contact with—those who harmed them. One of the biggest choices faced by survivors in this situation is how to navigate such proximity. Though it's often surprising to those providing support, not all survivors in relationships with someone who's harming them view leaving as the first step toward the rest of their lives. In this scenario, it's important for those providing support to remember that harm is often only one of several factors that a survivor has to take into account when choosing whether to stay or leave. The more external stability and shelter a pod can help a survivor access, the higher the likelihood the survivor will leave a situation where harm is ongoing, but remember that relationships are complex. We must not push a survivor to leave, or make them feel that our support is contingent on their decision to leave.

Jill Davies, director of the Building Comprehensive Solutions to Domestic Violence Initiative, explains the situation this way: If a survivor prioritizes providing for their family over leaving their situation, then "you wouldn't only offer strategies that would reduce financial security—for example, a shelter stay that would mean she loses her job or a move that would mean the loss of subsidized housing, or law enforcement that would mean her partner would lose the source of income that supports the family."[65] Help a survivor come up with as many long-term options as you can.

In our discussion of how to help a survivor stabilize on page 86, I told you about the Creative Interventions Risk Assessment Chart. If you've already helped a survivor fill out this chart, consider reviewing and updating it with their considerations about staying or leaving. If you haven't

....

65   Jill Davies, "Victim-Defined Safety Planning." 2017.
https://vawnet.org/sites/default/files/assets/files/2018-07/
Victim-Defined-Safety-Planning.1-17.pdf

helped them fill out the chart yet, doing so may help you get a better sense of the factors a survivor needs to weigh.

A survivor considering leaving may also want to think about creating what many social services and nonprofits call a "safety plan" (though to be honest, a much more fitting name for the ones I've seen online would be "exit checklist"). While they're fairly useless for safety planning, these checklists can be helpful for the survivor who's planning to leave or considering leaving, and who's organizing themselves toward that goal.

Most of these exit checklists assume the survivor is a woman in a heterosexual relationship, but in most cases, they're sufficiently generalized to apply to all genders. In addition, several LGBTQ-friendly organizations now maintain their own checklists, such as the National Coalition of Anti-Violence Programs[66] and FORGE[67]. More information is available online through a quick search with added keywords, such as: "financial safety plan domestic violence" or "legal safety plan California intimate partner violence."

Because leaving a situation of ongoing harm can be very dangerous, a survivor may decide to call on some or all of the additional resources that you helped them identify when you first mapped the pod. A number of organizations

....

66   National Coalition of Anti-Violence Programs, "Community Action Toolkit for Addressing Intimate Partner Violence Against People of Color," https://avp.org/wp-content/uploads/2017/04/ncavp_poc_ip-vtoolkit.pdf

67   FORGE, "Safety Planning: A Guide for Transgender and Gender Non-Conforming Individuals Who Are Experiencing Intimate Partner Violence," http://forge-forward.org/wp-content/docs/safety-planning-tool.pdf

and services do survivor advocacy and may be able to help with more personalized and useful safety planning. As with any other part of the process, if you or another pod member decide to help a survivor by reaching out to an organization or service, make sure that the survivor wants this assistance, and that the organization supports letting the survivor determine the course of action. Unfortunately, not all organizations responding to harm prioritize what a survivor wants or thinks is best for them. Some even mandate the involvement of law enforcement, so make sure you do your homework!

Tending to the Community

Tending to the community involves any actions taken to reduce the possibility that harm will recur, as well as efforts toward wider transformation so bystanders don't turn a blind eye or try to normalize harm.

Two methods of harm reduction that have become better known in the wake of #metoo are the *whisper network* and the *callout*. A whisper network is the backchannel through which community members share information with others they trust about people who have harmed. This kind of information sharing—though crucial in situations where the risk of retaliation is too high for a survivor to come forward—is limited in that it rarely reaches all members of a community. Though risky to the person making it, a callout is significantly more efficient at letting a community know that one of their members has harmed, others may be impacted, and the harm may recur. But callouts are not just the human spin on the mammalian alarm signal. They also present an invitation: for the person who harmed and for the community, and because of this, I consider callouts to be not only harm-reduction strategies, but also opportunities for transformation.

TRANSFORMATION

A callout is not the only way to catalyze transformation. A survivor may also explicitly ask the person who harmed them—either directly or through a pod member or other community member—to go through an *accountability process*. In an accountability process, a person who harmed is asked to take ownership of the impact of their actions and work with a pod of their own to examine their patterns and beliefs and begin the work to change. A survivor can participate in this process, or take a step back and let the community run the process (it is, after all, in the interest of a community to do what it can to minimize the risk of further harm). Sometimes, a person may notice they have harmed and initiate their own process with no initial community or survivor involvement. Accountability frameworks are extremely flexible, and processes undertaken in good faith are immensely powerful and transformational not only for people who harm, but also for those who step up to help. The change made possible by confronting harm together reverberates across an entire community.

There is no single way to do accountability but, in brief, a process generally involves an acknowledgment of the harm by the person who harmed, outlines a plan for the person who harmed to begin examining and changing their behavior, and defines ways to keep the community safe while the process continues (such as by asking the person who harmed to step down from positions of power or to disclose their harm to others in certain situations). In addition, a person who harmed may be asked to issue an apology and make reparations to the survivor, and even to the wider community.

Asking the person who harmed to step down from positions of power or disclose that they are in recovery for a certain type of harm is not done with the intention of shaming or punishing them. In fact, these requests are cooperative measures of harm reduction, since patterns of behavior may remain active even as a person who harmed begins working to change them. Likewise, reparations are not a form of punishment, but rather a way for the person who harmed to become an active participant in making positive change for those who were previously negatively impacted by their actions. The process is about change and integration, not punishment and isolation.

An accountability process is arduous work for those providing support to the person who harmed, who must both container that person's feelings and protect the community as the person who harmed wrestles with themselves. As a result, such a process is not offered by a community lightly—it takes immense love and faith for a group of people to undertake this amount of labor on someone's behalf. Though often characterized as angry or vengeful, a survivor who brings attention to the harm they experienced is a powerful catalyst in making such transformations possible. To learn more about holding an accountability process, I strongly encourage you to read the *Creative Interventions Toolkit*.

It is important to note that while an accountability process is something a survivor may choose to initiate, it is not *for* the survivor. An accountability process may involve things that a survivor finds validating or valuable—such as seeing their community and the person who harmed them acknowledge that harm happened—but it is not for the survivor. Catalyzing an accountability process for the person who harmed them does not "heal" a survivor. It does not undo the harm that happened. It certainly does not mean the survivor needs to stop talking about the harm they experienced, or that they should feel satisfied. An accountability process is an opportunity for the person who harmed to change, learn the impact of their actions, and do the work to ensure they do not harm again. It is a gift of transformation.

It's always possible that a person who harmed will not be ready to acknowledge the harm they caused, or that they'll lack the support of people who know how to help them overcome their internal resistance and container their impulse to retaliate when their harm is named. This possibility can make it risky for a survivor to come forward—not to mention extremely activating—which is one of the primary reasons that I delegate decisions about whether to call for accountability to Shape rather than encouraging it earlier in survivor support.

The best-case scenario is for a survivor to have support in place before initiating a callout. Even communities with a track record of initiating accountability successfully should aim for this goal, as community members can sometimes become so busy with making accountability happen that they leave the survivor unsupported. Another potential mis-step is when communities encourage the survivor to become deeply involved in the process, exposing them to activation every time the person who harmed them experiences a moment of resistance or acts out. Accountability processes can be tumultuous, even in cases that involve people who want to stop harming! Don't get me wrong—I don't think a survivor should be *barred* from the process. However, I think sometimes the emphasis placed on the process can lock a survivor out of exploring what their communities or groups of friends can do for them or with them to prioritize their increased or continued integration in that group.

CATALYZING ACCOUNTABILITY

If a survivor decides to call for accountability, they may choose to go about it in many ways—either by themselves or through someone else. We've already covered the callout as a method of calling for accountability, and another common method is the *call-in*. Both of these methods name the harm to the person who harmed and let them know action is need-ed. The difference lies in what is prioritized by those making the call for accountability. As mentioned previously, the callout prioritizes harm reduction and informed consent.

By naming a harm on a public medium, the person issuing the callout is not only letting the person who harmed know that accountability is needed, they're also informing the entire community about the harm.

A callout can double the work for folks who show up to support the person who harmed. Before an accountability process can begin, these folks must help the person who harmed work through shame spirals, retaliatory impulses, and other kinds of emotional resistance so the person who harmed can acknowledge their capacity for harm. Only then can the person who harmed own their actions and impact without minimizing, dismissing, deflecting, or denying. This initial phase of accountability support is hard even when there isn't a callout, but the public attention that follows one really turns the activation up a notch. On the other hand, callouts are unparalleled in helping expose bigger patterns, since they frequently encourage other survivors of the person who harmed to step forward.

Call-ins, on the other hand, prioritize safety cues when delivering the message to the person who harmed, in the hope that reducing activation will make them better able to listen and respond appropriately. A call-in, for example, is more likely to happen in private and face-to-face, through a friend of the person who harmed or in their company. Though call-ins happen in relative obscurity (and therefore may lack true community-wide harm-reduction qualities), they are acutely responsive to the nervous system cues of the person who harmed. This quality allows others to help the person who harmed regulate themselves, and reduces the risk of retaliatory behavior.

I'm never able to take a side in conversations about which of the two methods of calling for accountability is best—there are too many variables. Call-ins may be gentler and facilitate greater connection, but they also present an immense amount of emotional labor. There's no guarantee there won't be retaliation, and there is no bonus of safety in numbers. Certain patterns of harm can also limit who is able to safely make a call-in, so I disagree with folks who believe that one should always try a call-in before a callout. Both methods present their own sets of risks for the person issuing the call—especially if that person is the survivor. My answer is that it depends. I trust the body, and I trust that anyone considering issuing a call for accountability will do it in the way that feels safest for them.

An in-between method of asking for accountability is the *letter of concern*. This more formal approach takes more work to draft than a callout does, but it eliminates the real-time emotional labor of helping the person who harmed regulate themselves. Though such a letter may involve a number of signatories, it is generally directed only to the person who harmed and is therefore significantly more private than a callout. A letter of concern names the harm and briefly outlines what those signing hope for in terms of accountability.

A letter of concern that is made available to the public is an *open letter*. I categorize open letters as callouts since they name harm publicly.

The next time someone rags on Millennial "callout culture," you have my blessing to throw a newspaper or a Bible at them—from the op-ed to the Pauline epistles,[68] the callout has a long and rich history.

Letters of concern are not the only calls for accountability that make suggestions for or requests of the person who harmed. A regular callout can also include requests, and community-run accountability processes often make an effort to check in with survivors and their pods to see whether they hope the process will address anything in particular. What a survivor may decide to put into such a list is highly variable. I've seen requests from survivors and communities that were as simple as asking the person who harmed to acknowledge the harm and make an apology to the survivor, the community, or both. But requests may also be complex—for example, they may outline detailed steps a person who harmed might take to reduce the likelihood of additional harm as they undertake their process.

---

68   The Pauline epistles are a number of books in the Christian Bible that are attributed to Paul the Apostle. They summarize Paul's vision for how the church should operate, and a couple of them illustrate both naming harm and outlining steps to repair it.

I've heard people refer to such a list as a "list of demands," though I don't prefer the phrase, as it sounds rather like a kidnapping. In addition, I feel it can hurt a survivor badly if they're led to believe that a person who harmed can only achieve accountability if a survivor's wishes come to pass, or that empowerment for the survivor means getting the person who harmed to do whatever the survivor wants. Such beliefs can cause a lot of grief, especially in processes involving multiple survivors who make conflicting requests.

Accountability is the *recognition* by a person who harmed that harm was done, and the *taking of ownership* that is necessary for their internal transformation to unfold. We must help a survivor realize that a person who harmed may accept a process, take ownership of the harm they did, begin working to change their behavior to the satisfaction of a community, and yet not make good on any of the survivor requests that fall outside the process.

In my opinion, writing lists of requests for the person who harmed is most useful for survivors who want to repair their relationship with that person. This way, if the person who harmed wants to do repair, they can fulfill the requests to show good-faith intent and begin to rebuild trust with the survivor.

When a survivor doesn't want to repair their relationship with the person who harmed them, I feel that the list of requests is more effective when it's addressed to a community, group of friends, or peer network, outlining ways to ensure the survivor's continued integration. For example:

How can a community make sure the survivor is able to participate fully? How can its members help the survivor feel sheltered at events that may include the person who harmed them? What measures are being taken at events and gatherings to prevent additional harm?

Supporting Survivors: A Summary

As a survivor begins to process the harm they experienced, they will need increased support. As we've discussed, they may or may not process what happened immediately after the harm. Regardless of when this processing happens, a survivor will need to be witnessed, heard, supported, and sheltered. In this part, we covered some of the ways that friends can help a survivor regulate during periods of activation, as well as how to reestablish a baseline of internal safety so they can make some of the bigger decisions about their lives. Friends of a survivor can fill many roles during the weeks, months, and years that follow the processing of harm, and I hope that these chapters helped you get a better sense of the ways you can show up for your friend.

Remember: if you are human, you already have the toolkit to do this work.

Part II.
The Art of Caring for Ourselves

Chapter 5: Self-Care for Supporters

Showing up for people who have experienced harm or are trying to change harmful patterns is hard work! Just discussing the harm can cause activation, as can processing about harm and examining patterns of harm. Activation wears the body down—it interferes with digestion, sleep, and restoration, among other things—and this decreases our internal resources. The fewer our internal resources, the harder it is for us to meet those we're supporting with fortitude, receptivity, and compassion—three fundamental components in this work. In addition, burnout is correlated with a higher likelihood of secondary trauma, something I discuss at greater length later in this chapter. For this reason, engaging in self-care is absolutely crucial.

Ask a hundred people what the best form of self-care is and they'll come up with just as many answers. That makes sense—different bodies and minds have different needs, and different situations present different sets of options. What unites the answers is *discernment*, the mechanism through which we decide if the activity we've chosen is restorative.

Discernment is an embodied skill that uses *noticing* to consider our boundaries and refine our needs and limits.

Noticing

American society can be contradictory. We have vibrant security and preparedness cultures, and we take pride in the security systems we install for our homes. At the same time we treat feelings—especially hurt, fearful, and uncomfortable feelings—like they're weaknesses. It's almost as if we don't realize that feelings are the security systems we have for our bodies—and it does not get more state-of-the-art than our ability to take in hundreds of thousands of cues and react in fractions of a second! The human body is a sophisticated system comprised of countless instruments of detection, and feelings are essentially its push notifications.

It's a shame that we're not taught to inhabit these systems efficiently, and pay attention to the push notifications from our body like we do those from our phones. In fact, it's often the opposite: We think being fearless is some kind of power. We think it's a form of mastery to ignore our awareness of hunger, tiredness, and the need to use the bathroom. We think it's strong to push through our misgivings without paying them any attention. We have an incredible security system, and yet we pride ourselves on ignoring its alarms and being ignorant and disdainful of it.

To be present for friends and confront harm, we will need to undo this programming. Without our feelings, we're not in touch with our bodies' powerful detection systems, and we need to be in touch to do this work. Without our bodies, we don't know if we're actually okay with listening to a disclosure of harm from a survivor, or helping someone who harmed begin to examine their patterns. Without our bodies, we don't know our limits until we slam into them.

RECONNECTING

Connecting with how we feel after a lifetime of programming to the contrary is a wild ride, but my friend and transformational coach Arden Leigh showed me a hack to get greater awareness stat, which, if you can believe it, involves an app. Available on both Android and iPhone,[69] Mood Meter was developed by Yale's Center for Emotional Intelligence to help people to build self-awareness by assessing what they feel in their bodies on two scales: energy and pleasantness. It may feel silly, but thinking about emotions in this way makes it easier to notice them, and specifically, to pay attention to how we experience them in our bodies. If downloading an app feels a little over the top for you, that's okay. The only thing that developing emotional self-awareness absolutely requires is stopping for a minute to check in with yourself and ask: Is this feeling high or low energy? Is it pleasant or not pleasant? How does it feel in my body?

....

69   Mood Meter, http://moodmeterapp.com/science/

LEARNING

Several years ago, my friend and physical therapist Michael Takatsuno started working on my back and exclaimed, "Whatever you're doing, your body really doesn't like it!" I told him I wasn't doing anything physical that could be detrimental, to which he responded, "Well, what else are you doing?" As the founder of the Power Under Soft Hands (PUSH) system of muscle therapy, Michael has a deep understanding of the body, and he taught me how to start listening to mine. My body's recurring pattern of tension turned out to be self-protective[70]—a bracing against the outside while tightly containing me on the inside. I wasn't doing physically strenuous things I shouldn't have done. I was exposing my body to situations that impacted my internal sense of safety. But what were they?

In the process of learning myself, I began to recognize the many seemingly mundane body-related phenomena that were also talking to me: my breathing, my digestion, my ability to sleep and regulate my temperature, even my cravings (or the surprising absence of any cravings). But by far the most straightforward communicator among them was my heart.

....

70   The use of tension as defense, when chronic, is known as "body armoring." Elliot Greene and Barbara Goodrich-Dunn, *The Psychology of the Body* (Philadelphia: Lippincott Williams & Wilkins, 2013).

Thanks to the quantified self[71] movement, I easily acquired one of those devices that athletes wear on their wrists to monitor how well they're reaching their target heart rate for efficient calorie burning. The monitor I found let me set a threshold, which I did as soon as I established a baseline for myself. The following weeks were mind-blowing as the little device notified me of changes in my heart rate, inviting me to question how I *really* felt about the things I was doing, saying, thinking, and more. As it turned out, Michael was right: I was doing a lot of things my body didn't actually like, and once I actually stopped and thought more carefully about them, neither did I. My mind caught up to my body quickly once I reconnected myself: after two weeks, I took off the bracelet to charge it and realized that I could detect changes in my heart rate on my own.

Your body talks to you, too.

Discernment

Reconnecting to ourselves gives us access to a whole dashboard of gauges, but before we can use them, we need to familiarize ourselves with how to read them. One of my favorite tools for this process is what the psychologist Eugene T. Glendin called *focusing*. Focusing "is a process in which you make contact with a special kind of internal bodily

....

71   Gary Wolf, "Know Thyself: Tracking Every Facet of Life from Sleep to Mood to Pain, 24/7/365," *Wired,* June 22, 2007. https://www.wired.com/2009/06/lbnp-knowthyself/

awareness, I call this awareness *a felt sense*."[72] In his ground-breaking 1978 book on the subject, Glendin elaborates:

> *Focusing is not a process in which you "face" painful emotions nor one in which you sink down into them and risk drowning. Conversely, it is not an intellectual or analytical process either. [...] A felt sense is not a mental experience but a physical one. Physical. A bodily awareness of a situation or a person or event. An internal aura that encompasses everything you feel and know about the given subject at a given time—encompasses it and communicates it to you all at once instead of detail by detail. Think of it as a taste if you like, or a great musical chord that makes you feel a powerful impact, a big round feeling. A felt sense doesn't come to you in the form of thoughts or words or other separate units, but as a single (though often puzzling and very complex) bodily feeling.*

Sitting with the felt sense, turning it over without trying to rationalize what it is or talk ourselves out of it, is at the heart of Glendin's focusing. No matter how difficult the truth the body reveals to us, there's always a relief in being in our knowing. And in this knowing, discernment becomes possible. Discernment is what allows us to answer whether we're *really* able to be present for a friend who has experienced harm or harmed another, whether we need to pause to take care of ourselves, whether we can remain a core part of a

---

72   Eugene T. Glendin, *Focusing* (New York: Bantam, 1978).

pod or need to switch to a supporting role for a time or take a break from a process altogether.

BOUNDARIES AND LIMITS

No discussion of discernment is complete without a mention of boundaries. But before we get to it, I am going to do something I don't much enjoy doing and insist on a technicality. It's very common to use the terms *boundaries* and *limits* interchangeably. A boundary, most of us might agree, is what we do not want, what we're not okay with. This definition isn't bad, but my life has been so greatly enriched by Betty Martin, who differentiates between the two, that I must share her explanation with you.

Betty Martin is the cofounder of the School of Consent and the world's foremost educator on consent. Her model of the *domain* explicitly differentiates between boundaries and limits. "Our domain is what we have a right to and a responsibility for," she writes.[73]

> It includes our bodies, desires and feelings. What is in our domain does not change. We are always responsible for the things in it. With this understanding, we can define boundaries as the edge of our domain. Your boundary is what delineates what is inside your domain from what is not. A limit is what you are willing

---

73   Betty Martin's upcoming (as yet untitled) book about the Wheel of Consent details the elegant two-dimensional model of consent that she has been refining for the past twelve years.

to participate in and what you are not. A limit is your No. You have some limits you will not do at all, for anyone, ever, and other things you are available for depending on who it is, what the situation is, or how tired you are. You might set a limit today and change it for tomorrow, or five minutes from now. So limits change and this is a good thing.

In her model of the domain, limits are situational and highly context-dependent, whereas boundaries remain consistent. This model elegantly resolves the problem caused by discussions about boundaries as things that need to be set—as though the right to our bodies, for example, does not exist, and we need to take action with every person we meet to establish that they cannot act upon us however they please. This model also allows for fuller human expression, leaving space for the existence of contradictions, such as the need to be loved and the fear of intimacy.

When we view boundaries as the edges of our domains, we are better able to visualize where we end and others begin. When we know where we end and others begin, we can discern when a blaze on the horizon is not our fire and, though it may seem counterintuitive, this makes us significantly more reliable for others. When we know what fires we're responsible for, we can better forecast our bandwidth, allowing us to sign up to help others with their fires with intention. Knowing about our bandwidth and making commitments with intention helps us build trust with others, who learn that we are dependable when we make commitments. They can trust that we won't unknowingly spread ourselves so thin that we'll be forced to bail from burnout when they need us most.

WE DON'T KNOW WHAT WE DON'T KNOW

In pod work, it's very common to hear how important it is to be clear about our limits, but I'm not going to do that. If you haven't done support work or confronted harm before, how can you know what your limits are? You may not even have a clear idea where the edge of your domain is just yet!

Instead, I'm going to tell you that your limits matter. They matter even if you smash into them in the middle of a process and didn't make them clear before you started. Your limits matter. You are allowed to have them. You are sovereign.

You are sovereign.

I've noticed that when we fail to take on supporting roles with choice and agency, we can become extremely reactive when we discover we have limits so I'm going to say it once more: You are sovereign.

I could tell you to go gently and remind yourself that everyone in the process is doing the best they can, but I know our nervous systems don't work that way. Sometimes we get activated. It happens. Sometimes, we're running low on resources and we fall off an edge. Other times, it's bigger, like a trigger that brings up our own history with harm. When we're in these states, the advice to "assume best intentions" is no good. The body doesn't assume—it gets safe. You don't argue with a body—not the survivor's and not your own. In these moments, our bodies need to feel that we have choice, and that others recognize our individual right to take a break or leave if our bodies need it.

In an ideal world, we would move into every situation knowing our limits and communicating them clearly and eloquently. While I encourage us all to work for that world, I also want us to remember to be kind to ourselves on our way there. We don't know what we don't know. This is why I warn not to do support work alone. You need to be able to take a break or take a step back from the process and that's easier to do when you have established a group of people who are, at the very least, capable of providing emotional support to the survivor or the person who harmed.

Go slowly and with sovereignty. Take your time to decide whether you can accept pod work that comes up. Are you clear on what is being asked of you? Is it something you think you can do right now, at this stage in your life, given your emotional bandwidth? Under what conditions might you be better able to help with this task? Is the task something that may cause some activation for you, such as discussing harms? If so, what limits can you preemptively place to give yourself time to regulate and recover? Are there other pod members or resources, such as therapists, who can help you balance the load?

It is a lot easier to name our limits with grace and calm before we're right up against them, but if you do find yourself right up against yours, I want you to take a moment to tell yourself the following: *My limits keep me safe. I have a choice in this situation. Choosing to step back and take care of myself is responsible, and others know and recognize this. They do not expect me to set myself on fire to keep them warm. They may experience disappointment, and that is natural and valid. Their feelings are their domain. In taking a time-out, I am taking care of my domain, which is my responsibility as well as my right.*

Only when we're sovereign in ourselves is it possible to fully embody the compassion necessary to tell others that we need to modify our commitment to the pod. Telling others we need to take a step back will be hard for them to hear. A good way to do it is by taking ownership, which minimizes the likelihood of activation. It can be tempting to try to evade responsibility when we know others will be disappointed, so you'll have to be brave! Consider saying something like: "Some things are coming up internally that I was not expecting, and I need to take a step back and take care of myself. I am not able to verbalize what's going on for me right now, but I want you to know that you didn't do anything wrong."

If possible, let others know when they can expect to receive an update. For instance, "I'm going to take the next two weeks to let myself process what this is about. At that time, I'll message you to let you know how I am doing and whether I need to take a more permanent time-out." Though many of us have a tendency to do the opposite, in this line of work, it is a *lot* better to underpromise and overdeliver. Our courage to show our vulnerability allows others who depend on us to prepare. "Prepare for the worst, hope for the best," is how my friends in public relations put it.

When first doing support work, it's easy to mistake a state of reactivity for a crisis situation. It's not that reactivity is an imagined threat whereas crisis is a real one—both are very real things to the persons experiencing them. The difference is that a crisis requires better knowledge of a situation and more than a single person, whereas helping someone regulate activation is something a single person can do without necessarily knowing details of the harm or the pattern of harm. A crisis may call for all hands on deck, but activation can be delegated. You don't have to do it all yourself—and you *shouldn't*.

Recharging

Now that we've covered how to better notice ourselves and use that noticing to exercise discernment in our actions, we can move on to effective methods of recharging. After all, even the most self-aware and discerning person who undertakes this work is going to run into difficult situations and experience activation and exhaustion. The recharging toolkit is huge, but in general it tends to include ways to regulate and recalibrate internal safety.

SUPPORT SYSTEM

You're going to need your own group of people to help you regulate. I'm not going to tell you to find yourself a therapist, or that you now have to hold weekly extremely serious processing sessions with a trusted friend. No, what I want is for you to commit to making time to *enjoy* being with your friends. I want you to be proactive in making time to be with people who aren't likely to need your help regulating and plan fun things to do with them. Enjoying good times with other humans is a crucial way to stay regulated, avoid burnout, and make sure you're at your best for support work.

We must support those among us who have been hurt and help those who have harmed do the work to change, but we need to be mindful that we don't allow harm to become the center of our lives. As Laura van Dernoot Lipsky writes in her treatise on the importance of mindfulness for first responders and activists:

> *People may come to believe that feeling happy or lighthearted is a betrayal of all the countless humans, creatures, and environments that are under siege on this planet. They may act as if the only way they can express solidarity with suffering of any kind is by suffering themselves. [...] My work for trauma stewardship starts with each of us as individuals. This emphasis comes from my personal belief, rooted in life experience and years of study and professional practice, that our capacity to help others and the*

environment is greatest when we are willing, able, and even determined to be helped ourselves.[74]

You need your own life to continue, and you need to find a way to ensure that it continues as fully as possible. That means learning to trust folks you're podding with and delegating tasks so you don't take on everything yourself. It means preemptively setting limits for how much time you spend on work directly related to harm. It means helping those you're supporting find and access resources and tools that they can use on their own. Most importantly, it means encouraging closeness and enjoyable experiences both within the pod and outside of it.

It's important to be proactive, as it's easy to miss cues alerting us to a personal limit when we're not fully conversant with our bodies. Laurie Leitch, a psychotherapist who did trauma relief work in Thailand following the 2004 tsunami, explains: "As you care for people with your heart wide open, you often don't realize how much of what you are exposed to is being taken in and held in the body. It isn't until later that your body starts to let you know. I thought I was fine over there."[75] This situation is another reason why I recommend calling on others to help with support work, rather than trying to take it all on by ourselves, why I stress

....

74   Laura van Dernoot Lipsky and Connie Burk, *Trauma Stewardship: An Everyday Guide to Caring for Self While Caring for Others* (Oakland, CA: Berrett-Koehler Publishers, 2009).
75   van Dernoot Lipsky and Burk, *Trauma Stewardship*.

the importance of pod work that's not directly related to the harm, and why I want you to get *yourself* some support.

Studies of professionals in survivor advocacy and support have found a strong correlation between burnout and secondary trauma.[76] To better explain secondary trauma—or what psychologists Lisa McCann and Laurie Anne Pearlman call *vicarious traumatization*[77]—I'm going to borrow Laura van Dernoot Lipsky's analogy of the pond. Imagine harm as a stone cast into a pond, where "the initial impact creates repercussions that expand almost infinitely, reaching and having an effect on many people who didn't experience the [harm] beforehand."[78] A survivor's direct experience of harm causes traumatic stress, which can metastasize into the chronic condition we call post-traumatic stress disorder. Anyone who sees the harm happen can also develop signs of traumatic stress, as can those of us who hold space for accounts of harm by listening.[79] This is the

....

76   K. Shoji et al., "What Comes First, Job Burnout or Secondary Traumatic Stress? Findings from Two Longitudinal Studies from the U.S. and Poland," *PLoS ONE* 10, no. 8 (2015): e0136730, https://doi.org/10.1371/journal.pone.0136730

77   I.L. McCann and L.A. Pearlman, "Vicarious Traumatization: A Framework for Understanding the Psychological Effects of Working With Victims," *Journal of Traumatic Stress* 3, no. 1 (1990): 131–149, https://link.springer.com/article/10.1007/BF00975140

78   van Dernoot Lipsky and Burk, *Trauma Stewardship*.

79   Rachel Lev-Wiesel and Marianne Amir, "Secondary Traumatic Stress, Psychological Distress, Sharing of Traumatic Reminisces, and Marital Quality Among Spouses of Holocaust Child Survivors," *Journal of Marital and Family Therapy* 27, no. 4 (2001): 433–444, https://doi.org/10.1111/j.1752-0606.2001.tb00338.x

ripple of secondary trauma.[80] It makes sense that burnout and secondary trauma have a strong correlation. If you're burned out, you're not going to be able to regulate yourself well, and if you can't do that, then you can't help regulate someone else, either. And if that someone else is really activated, well, there's only one way your autonomic nervous system can go.

Our bodies are powerful instruments. We must take care of them and keep them calibrated.

BODY HACKING

Somatic therapists and bodyworkers have contributed a number of exercises to the body-hacking toolbox to help us calm an activated nervous system and even do the human equivalent of a hard reset. The following are a handful of resources that have helped me. As you explore these tools, please listen to your body and do not push yourself to try or finish any activity that does not feel good or right to you. Remember, we are different and what works for me may not feel good to you or may have unexpected consequences.[81] Tread with care.

Some of us get into support work without awareness of our own trauma and, sometimes, pod work can bring it to the

....

80   RW. Motta, "Secondary Trauma," *International Journal of Emergency Mental Health and Human Resilience* 10, no. 4 (2008): 291-298, https://www.ncbi.nlm.nih.gov/pubmed/19278145
81   In *Waking the Tiger*, Peter A. Levine recounts causing a panic attack in a client he tried to help with a relaxation technique. Her muscle tension had been helping her manage her feelings.

fore. If you suspect that your activation is disproportionate to the apparent cause, consider taking a pause from support work to check in with yourself. I recommend giving yourself at least two weeks to work through the activation and reach clarity. If you return to pod work and the issue persists, I encourage you to look for a safe way to work through what you're holding. If you cannot access a therapist, consider exploring the following tools and doing the exercises in order, rather than jumping around as I do below.

Levine's Twelve Phases

Peter A. Levine pioneered the somatic experiencing model for releasing trauma. Based in biology, the model understands trauma as energy that was locked in the body during danger and missed its opportunity to discharge. After the success of his first book describing his model and methods, Levine wrote *Healing Trauma: A Pioneering Program for Restoring the Wisdom of Your Body,* a short book detailing simple exercises that he uses to help his clients process trauma.

Several of Levine's exercises have been valuable in helping me recalibrate after activation, particularly his tapping exercise for "Finding Your Own Boundaries," in which you use your hands to tap on various areas of your body to reestablish connection with and ownership of it. Tapping on myself serves as a reminder of what is and is not my domain. I've used this technique in situations of activation, too, tapping my fingers on myself, thinking: *this is my body, and this is its physical boundary.*

Healing Trauma is available in print (and comes with a CD for those who prefer being guided through the exercises with audio rather than by reading), electronically on Kindle, and as audio on Audible. A number of Levine's exercises appear for free on YouTube, courtesy of the National Institute for the Clinical Application of Behavioral Medicine (NICABM), as well as by searching for "Peter Levine exercises."

TRAUMA RESILIENCY MODEL

The Trauma Resiliency Model (TRM), developed by Laurie Leitch and Elaine Miller-Karas,[82] is most commonly used as psychological first aid in response to extremely activating events, such as natural disasters.[83] TRM consists of several exercises that draw on the work of Peter Levine and Eugene Gendlin, both of whom we've discussed, as well as that of Anna Jean Ayres, including her sensory integration theory, which models how we take in sensory stimulation, organize it without becoming overwhelmed, and respond adaptively. You can learn the TRM exercises through the app iChill, which is available for free on iPhone, Android, and the

....

82   Laurie Leitch and Elaine Miller-Karas, "It Takes a Community," *Psychotherapy Networker,* November/December 2010, https://www. thresholdglobalworks.com/pdfs/it-takes-a-community.pdf
83   Linda Grabbe and Elaine Miller-Karas, "The Trauma Resiliency Model: A "Bottom-Up" Intervention for Trauma Psychotherapy," *Journal of the American Psychiatric Nurses Association* 24, no. 1(2017), doi: 10.1177/1078390317745133

web,[84] as well as in training from the Trauma Resource Institute.[85]

The TRM technique for grounding is one of my go-tos. It uses sensation to keep one anchored in the present. For example, if you are standing, the exercise suggests that you shift your attention to your feet and the ground under them. If you're sitting, you focus on the way the chair or sofa is supporting your body. The simple act of moving the attention away from what's causing distress and focusing it on sensation—especially a sensation of physical support—can be immensely powerful in moments of activation.

As with Levine's Twelve Phases tool, the TRM app iChill offers text as well as audio for users who prefer to be guided through the exercises that way. You can also find various videos on YouTube explaining some of the exercises by searching for the phrase "trauma resiliency model."

OTHER TOOLBOXES

Many exercises have been developed over the past twenty years to help people apply a brake to their survival responses and activation, and the self-help aisle is full of them. What follows is a non-comprehensive list of helpful books I've picked up over the years. I'll leave it to you to determine what works for your body and situation.

....

84   iChill, 2019, http://www.ichillapp.com/info.html
85   Trauma Resource Institute, "TRM Trainings," 2019, https://www.
traumaresourceinstitute.com/trm-trainings/

The book *Somatic Psychotherapy Toolbox: 125 Worksheets and Exercises to Treat Trauma and Stress* by Manuela Mischke Reeds offers exercises similar to those pioneered by Levine and presented in the TRM. Similarly, the workbook *101 Trauma-Informed Interventions* by Linda A. Curran provides a number of exercises for managing activation and overwhelm. Both of these texts provide short explanations about each exercise, but don't elaborate on the mechanisms involved. To learn more about those mechanisms, a much better text is Peter Levine's *In an Unspoken Voice: How the Body Releases Trauma and Restores Goodness*, as well as *The Body Remembers Casebook: Unifying Methods and Models in the Treatment of Trauma and PTSD* by Babette Rothschild.

Exercises more tailored to help you cope with overwhelm can be found in *The Dialectical Behavioral Therapy Skills Workbook* by Matthew McKay, Jeffrey C. Wood, and Jeffrey Brantley, especially chapters one through seven, which deal with distress tolerance, emotional regulation, and mindfulness. For those whose responses to activation tend toward checking out, the workbook *Coping With Trauma-Related Dissociation* by Suzette Boon, Kathy Steele, and Onno van der Hart may be more useful, especially chapter 18, which deals with expanding one's window of tolerance and learning to regulate oneself.

Lastly, I'll mention some smartphone apps that put resources right into our pockets. Calm,[86] which is available for iPhone and Android, offers voice-guided body scanning,

---

86   Calm, 2019 https://calm.com

emergency self-soothing, and other relaxation techniques. Calm is free to download with limited functionality—for example, you are only able to do one of each type of guided meditation—but it's more than enough to get a sense of how the app works and whether the monthly fee is worth your while. If the expense doesn't suit your budget or you have no interest in downloading another app, look for "guided meditation" on YouTube, Spotify, or the app you use to listen to podcasts or audiobooks, and see what's available.

A different kind of app I've been exploring harnesses modern technology for bilateral stimulation. Several of these apps exist on the market, all of which base themselves to some extent on the work of psychologist Francine Shapiro, who in the late 1980s noticed that quick eye movements seemed to reduce the anxiety generated by intrusive thoughts.[87] Now a better-researched treatment for trauma called Eye Movement Desensitization and Reprocessing therapy (EMDR), its core component of bilateral stimulation has expanded from eye movements to audio and tactile cues. Smartphones are able to easily reproduce auditory cues, as well as visual ones to some extent. If tactile stimulation seems more promising for you, the Utah company Bi-Tapp offers tactile devices, and Laurel Parnell's *Tapping In: A Step-by-Step Guide to Activating Your Healing Resources*

87   Ramon Landin-Romero, Ana Moreno-Alcazar, Marco Pagani, and Benedikt L. Amann, "How Does Eye Movement Desensitization and Reprocessing Therapy Work? A Systematic Review on Suggested Mechanisms of Action," *Frontiers in Psychology*, 9, 2018: 1395, doi: 10.3389/fpsyg.2018.01395

Through Bilateral Stimulation provides instructions for manual stimulation.

> If psychology isn't something you're comfortable work-
> ing with, you might wander deeper into the self-help
> side of the aisle, or turn to your culture or your faith
> for resiliency-building tools. In the book *Psychological
> Trauma*, trauma specialist Bessel van der Kolk outlined
> the four most important factors for stress resistance:
> social support, a sense of control, pursuit of meaningful
> tasks, and a diversity of healthier coping and relaxation
> mechanisms. If you find it helpful to do things that have
> not been explained by science and they do not harm
> you or anyone else, then do them. Anything that creates
> an increased felt sense of safety has the power to help
> us shift. As my husband once quipped, butchering the
> words of the futurist Arthur C. Clarke, "Any sufficiently
> advanced magic is indistinguishable from psychology."

Restart and Hard Reset

As I mention in the discussion of stimulation, you can use the body to help your nervous system stabilize itself. Another well-known method for this strategy is the Tension and Trauma Release Exercises (TRE) series, which was developed by David Berceli to help people release the tension created in the body by activation. These stretches induce a shaking response that allows the body to release muscular tension.

TRE workshops are offered around the world by different organizations, and many of them also certify providers in professions as varied as yoga instruction, massage therapy, and life coaching. A search for your state or country along with the keyword "TRE" will help you find what's available in your area.

TRE instructional videos are also available for free on YouTube by searching "tension release exercises," though do take care, as it's not always clear whether the person you're watching has trained in this method. I also recommend that you don't try TRE alone. I've never had any strong reactions from TRE, but I've seen them happen—release can be emotional for some people.

I refer to TRE as a system restart because even though I tear up a little sometimes while doing the stretches, they don't prevent me from returning to regular functioning. For more of a "hard reset," you could try Stanley Rosenberg's Basic Exercise, which he describes as activating the ventral vagus nerve[88] to allow your nervous system to return to social engagement. Rosenberg's Basic Exercise, as described in his book *Accessing the Healing Power of the Vagus Nerve*, is wonderfully simple. You need five minutes and just enough room to lie on your back (though eventually you can do it sitting up). Before you lie down, bring your hands to the back of your head and interlace your fingers as though you're about to do classic crunches. Lower your body to the

....

88   Stanley Rosenberg, *Accessing the Healing Power of the Vagus Nerve: Self-Help Exercises for Anxiety, Depression, Trauma, and Autism* (Berkeley, CA: North Atlantic Books, 2017).

floor and allow yourself to feel your head cradled by your hands, your fingers pressed against your skull. Now, without turning your head, move your eyes to the right and keep them there until you experience a release in the form of a deep breath, a sigh, or a yawn. This can sometimes take up to thirty seconds. (If you feel distressed, try the left side first and come back to the right side once you experience release on the left.) Do the exercise on both sides. When both sides have released, bring your eyes back to center, take a breath, and slowly get up.

This simple exercise applies what Stephen W. Porges refers to as the "ventral brake" on the autonomic nervous system, halting activation. I call it a hard reset because it has the power to clear everything—but that also means it takes a bit of time to load the last backup, if you'll forgive me for overextending the metaphor. Possibly because the ability to concentrate requires a smidge of activation, this exercise turns me into something of a space case for a good several hours. It can also be digestively stimulating—expect some movement within the next four or so hours.

Another body hack that I've not personally tried yet is the Safe and Sound Protocol (SSP), an intervention developed by Stephen W. Porges that uses sound-based safety cues to reduce stress and bring the body back to a state of social engagement. Made commercially available in the United States through the neurotech company Integrated Listening Systems, or iLs, the intervention involves listening to music specifically processed to maximize auditory safety cues for forty-five minutes, five days in a row. Studies on the efficacy and applications of SSP (which is largely referred to in the literature by its original name "Listening Project Protocol") are ongoing.

Note of Caution: Trauma Mastery

In their book *Trauma Stewardship,* Laura van Dernoot Lipsky and Connie Burk explain the ongoing issue of trauma mastery for professionals whose work routinely brings them in contact with harm and other dangers. Trauma mastery is the revisiting of a traumatic incident in an attempt (not always conscious) to change the outcome. Those of us who intervene in harm are not immune.

"We seek to turn a traumatic situation in which we once felt powerless into a new situation where we feel competent and in charge," they write. "This is a sophisticated coping mechanism and by and large it is done unconsciously. If we are conscious that we are seeking trauma mastery, and if we navigate with insight, mindfulness, and honesty, this mechanism may contribute to our healing. More often, though, our attempts at trauma mastery lack awareness and intention."

If you're aware of a history of harm in your life, I invite you to begin examining how you are attending to it in yourself. We are more capable when we attend to ourselves, rather than when we attempt to use others as vehicles for our healing. This is true whether the person we're supporting is a survivor or the person who harmed. A survivor needs to reconnect with their sovereignty to establish greater internal safety. This means they need to make their own decisions, even if you don't agree with them. There is no control for you to take here: their path is theirs. The person who harmed, meanwhile, may take a long while to fully examine their patterns and follow them back to their point of origin. The process is tumultuous and long—in many cases, it is lifelong. A person who harmed may flee and return to their process many times. Some do not return for months, even years. It does not serve us to pin our healing on that of others. And we do not need to.

Attend to your wounds. You can heal, and you are worthy of healing.

Part III:
When Your Friend Has Harmed

Chapter 6: Friendship Has Power

If you recently learned that your friend harmed or may have harmed someone else, you're probably experiencing a lot of different feelings. There's shock and disbelief, the inability to reconcile both the good they've done in your life and the harm they've caused in someone else's. There is also worry and the fear of complicity—that you may have inadvertently been party to harm or colluded with your silence about things you noticed that didn't feel quite right. There's also betrayal: you trusted your friend and vouched for them to others, and in harming, they seriously injured that trust. And under this tumult of feelings, there's also the relationship you've built with your friend. The person who harmed may be someone you've known for years, someone you care about a lot.

Navigating all of these feelings is hard and it's made more complicated by sensing that we need to do something but not knowing what. When we don't know what to do, we can't be of help and may even do things that—while meant to help—only contribute to the harm. The inability to cope could make us try to smooth things over by refusing the possibility that harm could have happened in the first place. The fear of having to make a break with someone we care about could lead us to characterize a cry for help from a survivor as an attack. Not knowing what to do can cause us to act in ways that are not in integrity with our values.

Fortunately for us, others have walked this path before us. We can follow their trail markers. We can learn what to do so we can be useful to people we love when they harm. Because they *will* harm. Someone we love will harm, and so will we. Maybe it won't be one of the harms associated with #metoo, but those are not the only possible harms.

We will harm, and so too will our friends, our lovers, our family members, our mentors, our idols, and other people we care about. But I believe it's possible to work together to stop harm from compounding and to stop patterns of harm from continuing. It's possible for us to help one another see how our actions impact others, and find the courage to interrogate what drives these behaviors.

Doing this work asks much of us. We need courage to stand up to someone we love and tell them that their actions are not okay. We need strength to provide a container for them as they grapple with the truth and implications of their harm. We need perseverance to stand firm even as they lash out in their fear and shame. We need fortitude to protect others in our communities from harm as our friends make their journeys to change. We need patience as they walk their paths, and slip and rise and slip again. Most of all, we need to keep the faith.

We need to believe it's possible to help others change and transform. I know it's possible. I've seen people recognize their wrongs and examine their patterns so they can change them. I've seen people transform and grow. I have seen them go on to support survivors and other people who harmed, creating a ripple effect of greater resiliency to counter the ripples of activation and isolation that their harm caused. As Nora Samaran writes: "Violence is nurturance turned backward."[89]

I have also seen this transformation in myself. I wrote in the Introduction that I made many mistakes in learning how to support survivors and people who harmed. (And I'm still learning!) Some of my mistakes along the way caused very real harm. It is in owning that harm and examining how I may be doing similar things in other areas of my life that I have experienced the greatest change.

Think back for a moment and remember a time in your life where you recognized that you were doing something that wasn't good for others, and you decided to change. It doesn't matter if it was something you think of as a big or a small thing. The memory of that decision is your talisman. I want you to keep it close and look to it when you start to lose hope, so you can remember that though conscious change is hard, we do it all the time.

In the following pages, I'll show you more examples, not only of change, but change made possible by social support. Keep the faith. Silicon Valley taught me that hope is not a

....

89   Nora Samaran, *Turn This World Inside Out: The Emergence of Nurturance Culture* (Chico, CA: AK Press, 2019).

strategy, but transformative justice showed me that hope is a discipline.[90]

Here's the truth: our friends are going to break our hearts. But with our help and a lot of courage, they may also show us the incredible capacity of the human animal to learn, to change, and to grow.

Like a Friend

Studies continue to show that healthy social bonds have a significant impact on whether someone harms again—more so than deterrence through punishment. Many of these studies have been influenced by the work of Harry Nigh, a Canadian pastor in Hamilton, Ontario, who inadvertently created a framework for preventing harm when he invited Charlie Taylor—a man with a history of serious harm against minors—to Hamilton after his release from prison.

Nigh had no training in working with people who harmed. He knew Taylor from a religious program for inmates and decided to step up when a psychologist at the prison called to ask if he could help get Taylor a job. The psychologist hoped that a Mennonite farm would be suffi- ciently remote as to make it unlikely for Taylor to continue

....

90   I learned the phrase "Hope is a discipline" from Mariame Kaba (@prisonculture), "Before i log off. One thing. Many years ago, I heard a nun who was giving a speech say 'hope is a discipline.' It stuck with me and became a sort of mantra for me. I understood her to be saying that hope is a practice." Twitter, June 20, 2018, https://twitter.com/ prisonculture/status/1009621164241641473.

his pattern of harm.[91] The farm was not an option, so Nigh decided to recruit members of his congregation to help Taylor keep from harming.

Now called Circles of Support and Accountability, the setup for Taylor involved a group of five or six volunteers, one of whom checked in daily with Taylor, while others took turns on differente days. In addition, the whole group came together once a week. In lieu of a support system, the group that Nigh created for Taylor took on the functions of a group of friends: setting norms and providing support emotionally and materially. Taylor's group helped him find housing and a steady source of income, and made sure he was able to meet medical and court-mandated appointments. They listened when things got tough and hard feelings came up, giving support when they could and holding boundaries firmly but also with compassion.

Circles of Support and Accountability, or COSA, worked for Charlie Taylor, who lived the remaining twelve years of his life without any other reports of harm. It also worked for Wray Budreo—notorious in Canada for a violent history of harm—after another group was called together to help him following his release in Toronto.[92]

91   Harry Nigh, "COSA Testimonies," http://www.circles4.eu/about-cosa/cosa-method-volunteers-professionals-cirlces/testimonies/
92   Joan Delaney, "Sex Offender Support Circles Help Keep Communities Safe," *Epoch Times.* October 22, 2009. https://www.theepochtimes.com/sex-offender-communit_1520397.html

The idea of people coming together in response to harm is rooted in the traditions of peacemaking circles, which COSA references in its name, of the Indigenous peoples and First Nations of North America (Turtle Island). The best studied of these frameworks come from First Nations peoples of the Yukon, Saskatchewan, and Manitoba, as well as the Diné (Navajo) in the United States.[93] Specifics differ among nations and tribes, but in general, peacemaking circles enable a person who harmed to take ownership of their actions, a survivor to be witnessed, repair to unfold, and the integrity of the tribe to be restored. Because the emphasis is on maintaining the integrity of the tribe, this approach and others that are similar or based on it are known as *restorative justice*.

In the 1980s, in an effort to ensure First Nations involvement in the criminal justice process and to reduce state violence, a framework based on peacemaking circles was modified to work alongside the courts in Canada.[94] The modified framework was first implemented in the Yukon in 1991,[95] three years before the release of Charlie Taylor across the country in Hamilton, Ontario.

....

93   Search "Hollow Waters" for the First Nations model, and "Diné Peacemaking" for the Navajo one.
94   Heino Lilles, "Circle Sentencing: Part of the Restorative Justice Continuum," International Institute for Restorative Practices, August 9, 2002. https://www.iirp.edu/eforum-archive/4250-circle-sentencing-part-of-the-restorative-justice-continuum
95   Lynette Parker, "Circles," Lesson 3: Programs of Intro to Restorative Justice, Centre for Justice & Reconciliation, http://restorativejustice.org/restorative-justice/about-restorative-justice/tutorial-intro-to-restorative-justice/lesson-3-programs/circles/#sthash.BCjGGWcq.dpbs

Nigh, then, was not the first to do this kind of work, nor was his process the most sophisticated, but what he contributed to the dialogue has profound implications for individuals with weaker social ties, like many of us in modern society. A community as tightly knit as a tribe can confront harm and take measures to stop it from continuing, and so can relative strangers. All it takes to stop harm, Nigh and his volunteers showed, is a group of people willing to check in and show up—to *act* like friends.

THE TRUE STATE OF BEING HUMAN

The solutions that humanity has ideated and the frameworks we've built to confront harm are a forest. Some frameworks are like the aspen, growing in parallel and sharing a root system. Others stand close together, but share only the soil that is our embodied need for safety. I will not tell you that I know all of these frameworks, or even most—though I would like to—but I can tell you about some of the ones that have shaped my way of thinking, given me hope when things were hard, and guided my way.

Restorative justice was not new in New Zealand when, in 1989, the juvenile justice system adopted a model[96] based on the historic practices of the Māori. Seven years earlier, in 1982, the former professional rugby player Mita Mohi had shown the transformative power of community-building

....

96   Fred W.M. McElrea, "Twenty Years of Restorative Justice in New Zealand," *Tikkun*. January 10, 2012, https://www.tikkun.org/newsite/twenty-years-of-restorative-justice-in-new-zealand

and traditional conflict-resolution practices through his trainings on the use of Māori weaponry. His program for at-risk youth was founded on *whanaungatanga*, a Māori word that describes the bonds we forge through shared experience—bonds that confer a sense of deep belonging and responsibility to one another.[97] By bringing together teens and Māori role models for the multi-day trainings, Mohi facilitated lasting connections and greater community integration, demonstrating the role that those with social capital can play in the process of transformation.[98]

The same conclusions echo through the work[99] of Tage Rai, whose research focuses on the morality of violence. "If [individuals'] primary social groups make them feel that they should not be violent, they won't be," Rai concludes in a piece summarizing several years of his work on the use of violence to regulate social relationships.[100]

At the time that Mita Mohi began his trainings in New Zealand, a different approach with a similar objective was already underway across the world in the United States as part of a collaboration between inmates and Quakers in New

---

97   "whanaungatanga," Māori Dictionary, https://maoridictionary.
co.nz/word/10068
98   Kim Workman, "Restorative Justice in a Māori Community,"
E-Tangata, November 18, 2018, https://e-tangata.co.nz/reflections/
restorative-justice-in-a-maori-community/
99   Tage Shakti Rai and Alan Fiske, "Moral Psychology is Relationship
Regulation: Moral Motives for Unity, Hierarchy, Equality, and
Proportionality," *Psychological Review* Vol 118(1), Jan 2011: 57-75,
https://doi.org/10.1037/a0021867
100   Tage Rai, "How Could They?" Aeon, June 18, 2015, https://aeon.
co/essays/people-resort-to-violence-because-their-moral-codes-
demand-it

York. That effort would eventually become the Alternative to Violence Project (AVP), with workshops taught in thirty-five states and fifty countries around the world.

The 1971 Attica Prison Uprising had inadvertently brought together a group of community organizers and political prisoners at Green Haven Correctional Facility. The Think Tank, as the group came to be called, included Edwin Ellis, a former leader of the New York Black Panther Party,[101] and immediately set to work developing mutual aid programs for the inmates. The group's chief concern was the young inmates who arrived at Green Haven for minor offenses, left, and returned over and over for increasingly serious crimes. To break the cycle, the Think Tank focused on helping inmates strengthen their relationships, both on the inside and beyond the prison walls. First, they created peer support groups to complement mutual aid efforts. Then, they called in the Quakers.

The Quakers—or the Society of Friends, as they are formally known—have historically been involved in prison reform and nonviolence work. Since at least the 1960s, they had been active in conflict resolution, which made them a natural fit for collaboration with the Think Tank. The Friends agreed, and drawing on earlier Quaker nonviolence initiatives and lessons from the American Civil Rights Movement, the coalition of minds began to develop what would become the AVP. The first workshop

....

101   Valerie Linet, "The Classroom Inside: Green Haven Prison," *Vassar, the Alumnae/i Quarterly* (Spring 2002), https://vq.vassar.edu/issues/2002/02/features/classroom-inside.html

was implemented in 1975 with the assistance of civil rights activist Bernard Lafayette, and the program soon spread through New York State prisons and into communities and youth groups far beyond the prison system.

At the heart of the AVP is the idea of transforming power—our fundamental ability to transform any situation with our words and actions.[102] "Being connected is the true state of being human," reads the AVP Second Level manual.[103] "Transforming power is that force in the universe which shows us how to do that." This seemingly simple notion would become foundational for transformative justice efforts in later decades, which sought not only to *restore* a community after harm, but to approach harm as an opportunity to *transform* a society.

TRANSFORMATIVE JUSTICE

GenerationFIVE is recognized as being the first group to publish about how confronting harm makes social transformation possible. Founded in 1995 as runriot! by Staci Haines (who would go on to write *Healing Sex: A Mind-Body Approach to Healing Sexual Trauma* and to expand the field of somatics), the group's earliest incarnation focused on survivor activism. Within two years, the runriot! crew

....

102   AVP-USA, Inc., "What is the AVP Program?" 2019, https://avpusa. org/what-we-do/
103   AVP-USA. Inc., "Alternatives to Violence Project: Manual for Second-Level Course," 2005.

had joined organizers and leaders in queer, Black, Latinx,[104] Asian, and immigrant communities in the wider discussion of how best to address harm against children.

The dawn of the new millennium was a powerful time in the San Francisco Bay Area. In 2000, INCITE! Women of Color Against Violence—a network of radical feminists of color—held a conference in Santa Cruz that energized the dialogue about alternatives for justice. Many of the thinkers brought together by INCITE! participated in developing the concepts in the 2007 generationFIVE white paper *Toward Transformative Justice*. The paper describes the four goals of a transformative justice as:

1. Safety, healing, and agency for survivors
2. Accountability and transformation for those who harm
3. Response and accountability for the community
4. Transformation of the social conditions that create and perpetuate harm.

Mimi Kim, a founding member of INCITE! and collaborator on the generationFIVE white paper, founded Creative Interventions in 2004 to put those transformative justice principles into action. In 2012, Creative Interventions released an early online version of the *Creative Interventions Toolkit*, a complete step-by-step manual for intervening in harm. The Toolkit was instrumental in helping me see not only that change was possible, but how to make it happen.

....

104   "Latinx" is a gender-neutral term that refers to Latin American persons of all genders.

Without Creative Interventions, I could not have written this book.

Confronting Harm

The law is a core part of American society and it can be difficult for some of us who have grown up within it to see beyond it. When the only model we have for addressing wrongs is one in which people who harm are punished, and when the punishments doled out by the state are as serious as they are, an accusation of harm alone can feel like a threat—a threat of very, very real harm. After all, the only thing the state knows to do is punish, and the punishments are extremely vicious: denial of liberty (temporary or permanent), torture (solitary confinement, violence, denial of access to basic care, etc.), and death.

I don't blame us for recoiling at the thought of someone facing such outcomes, but it's possible to stand against prison-based solutions without sweeping harm under the rug. It is possible to help our friends consider their actions, examine their patterns, and commit to their own growth. And we don't have to wait for the initial whispers about harm to become a chorus of shouts. We can start now, as soon as we hear that something happened.

THE THINGS WE TELL OURSELVES

The harm *could* be an honest mistake, some kind of accident or misunderstanding. You would not be the first friend to want to believe that. But it could also be part of a pattern, something that has happened before and will happen again.

I've been on that tightrope. A lot of friends have. The people we trusted called the first survivor's story a lie, or minimized the harm as a one-time youthful indiscretion. They swept away our misgivings, leaving us to be crushed by the subsequent testimonies of other survivors. Our feeling of betrayal is overshadowed only by the heartbreak and horror we feel at our complicity. Those who haven't lived through that heartbreak have seen it unfold in the wake of #metoo, seen how one survivor breaks the silence to reveal a long line of others.

When we ignore whispers that a friend of ours has harmed, dismiss allegations as attacks, sit in silence as our friend talks about something they've done that sounds a heck of a lot like harm, we aren't being good friends. We aren't protecting them. Protecting someone means wanting the best for them, and sometimes wanting the best means asking uncomfortable questions. Sometimes being a good friend means taking action about things we've heard, and intervening when we hear something troubling.

THE MISSING STAIR

Cliff Jerrison coined one of the most important allegories about broken communities seven years ago when he wrote about the "missing stair."[105] Jerrison wrote that a person who is known to cause harm in a community is not unlike a structural danger in a house, like a missing stair. People who live in the house know about it and have developed methods to get around safely but those who visit are not always told about the stair or taught the workaround, and, as a result, they tend to get hurt.

After learning that someone with a history of harm was regularly invited to parties and community events, Jerrison posted about the situation on his blog. He was surprised when, despite not mentioning names, he received numerous emails from community members who knew exactly who he was talking about.

"I think there were some people in the community who were intentionally protecting him," Jerrison writes. "But there were more who were *de facto* protecting him by treating him like a missing stair. Like something you're so used to working around, you never stop to ask 'what if we actually fixed this?' Eventually you take it for granted that working around this guy is just a fact of life, and if he hurts someone, that's the fault of whoever didn't apply the workarounds correctly."

....

105   Cliff Jerrison, "The Missing Stair," Pervocracy, June 22, 2012, http://pervocracy.blogspot.com/2012/06/missing-stair.html

In some situations, confronting harm is not advisable and workarounds, like whisper networks, become the only tool for harm reduction. These situations can include cases involving extreme power imbalances, as well as ones where a survivor may be at risk of retaliation if the person who harmed learns they've disclosed. But much more often, people are forced to rely on whisper networks because someone is harming and their friends are not willing to call them in. When we don't recognize our responsibility to step up and help our friends stop harming, the "missing stair" workarounds described by Jerrison become the default.

Predators rely on community protection to silence victims. Far too often, our commitment to our political party, our religious group, our sport, our college, or a prominent member of our community causes us to choose to disbelieve or to turn away from the victim. Far too often, it feels easier and safer to see only what we want to see. Fear of jeopardizing some overarching political, religious, financial or other ideology—or even just losing friends or status—leads to willful ignorance of what is right in front of our own eyes.

—Rachael Denhollander, gymnast and survivor[106]

106   Rachael Denhollander, "The Price I Paid for Taking on Larry Nassar," *The New York Times*. January 26, 2018, https://www.nytimes.com/2018/01/26/opinion/sunday/larry-nassar-rachael-denhollander.html

THE PIT AND THE HARBOR

Humans are social mammals. When a friend of ours is harming and we pretend that everything is okay, others receive our cues that everything's fine. That means that even if we don't actively participate in the harm, even if we don't want to collude, we *still do*. I will never forget the words I read on an anonymous guest post[107] on the blog of Kelly Sundberg, author of the survivor memoir *Goodbye Sweet Girl*: "When you refuse to ostracize abusers like him, or act to make them take responsibility and help with their public accountability, you're helping them pull other people into their orbits. You may not want to admit this, but you are part of the problem. You are the leafy branches camouflaging the pit full of snakes and skeletons."

I would go further and say that we are complicit even when we don't know that a friend is harming. Our lack of knowledge doesn't change our status as leafy branches. There's still a snake pit there and we are still camouflaging it. When we interact with them in public, online or off, we signal to others that we see our friend as safe. That has consequences for others.

We've been saying "Oh my word, I had no idea!" for a long time. What will it take for us to recognize that creating a culture of accountability is an active role? We can't expect accountability culture to magically bloom in our

....

107   Anonymous, "Guest Post: The Branches That Cover the Snake Pit," Apology Not Accepted, August 10, 2017, https://kellysundberg.com/guest-post-the-branches-that-cover-the-snake-pit/

communities, in a society where most survivors default to silence. If we mean it when we say that we wish things were different, we need to do the work. This work begins not with our friends, but with us. How do we invite others to trust us? No one's going to tell you that something your bestie did seems iffy if you don't do the work to make it safe for people to tell you such things.

This work starts with talking about harm. It starts by recognizing that "I don't do drama" isn't a statement of chill, but one of collusion—it is a shruggie where our sense of responsibility should be.

This work calls on us to do drama. No one is going to come to us until we're willing to prioritize the safety of our communities. We need to be braver than we have been. We need to start talking about our position on harm and our commitment to accountability, even when it comes to ourselves and our friends.

Talking feels like such a small thing. Yet survivors take notice. When they see us talking about harm and accountability, and supporting other survivors publicly, they notice. Talking is how we begin transforming from a leafy branch covering the snake pit into a safe harbor.

THE WORDS WE USE

Some time ago, a friend came to me to thank me for supporting survivors. When I took the opportunity to call him in for not being more active in holding members of our community accountable for their harm, he told me something

I'll never forget: "I'm afraid that if I support a callout, I too will be excised from my community."

As startling as this leap of logic seems to be, it's not the first time I've heard it. When we relate to those harming more than we do to survivors, as so many of us do, it is easy to immediately imagine ourselves in *their* shoes instead of those of the survivor. Having said that, it is *also* true that callouts are catalyzing—not only do they mobilize other survivors of the person being called to account, they frequently bring forward survivors of harms done by others. It's why I like to think of accountability processes as opportunities for entire communities to clean house.

Aware of the possibility that my friend's worry might be driven by a genuine fear of being called to account for harm he had done, I took a breath and asked him why he thought that he would be ostracized.

"Isn't that what happens?" he asked me. "People say you harmed, and people get angry, and you get kicked out."

"It doesn't have to be that way," I told him. "You could have a process and own your harm and its impact on the other person, commit to not harming, offer reparations to the person you harmed and the community, and begin to examine whether the harm is part of a pattern in your life."

"I've never seen that happen," he said.

That day, I realized that how we talk about harm isn't only important for survivors, but also for people who harm. That day, I stopped referring to people by the harm they had done. A harm-*er*, a harm-*ist*—terms like these describe identity. Instead, I started using a phrase I'd learned from

Creative Interventions: *person who harmed*. At first, I didn't like using this phrase. It was clunky and awkward—and it's *still* clunky and awkward. But I like what it conveys. It says: you are not the things you do. It says: I believe in your ability to change. It says: I will do what I can to help you.

Our Friends, Our Business

Talking opens the gates. The more we discuss the importance of confronting harm, the more we signal our intention to receive information about harm in good faith. Here, we must prepare for the gift of disclosure, so we can respond appropriately when we learn of a callout or see one, and so we know what to do if a friend tells us that they harmed someone else.

BEING READY

Being ready to listen requires three things: fortitude, receptivity, and compassion. Learning that harm has happened is shocking, and hearing that someone we care about caused it will be profoundly upsetting. We must have the fortitude to allow our feelings to unfold inside us without hijacking our words and actions.

If you're not used to emotional management, the idea that we're able to separate feelings from reactions will seem daunting. Don't be discouraged! You can start practicing right now by committing to taking a breath before responding any time you start to feel annoyed or irritated. Social media is an excellent practice ground for expanding the window of time between activation and response. The next time you see an update that really annoys you, or a post that begs for correction, exit the app and do something else for a while. (When and if you do circle back, ask yourself: does this *actually* merit your time and energy?)

Cristien Storm writes powerfully about the pause that makes the difference between reacting and responding in her book *Living In Liberation*.[108] Storm writes: "The pause could be for any length of time [...] what is important is the pause itself. The pause signals to the body that one is not in immediate and impending danger."[109] When we take the time to pause, we allow our feelings to exist without clouding our intention, which in this case is to be present and learn everything we can about what has happened.

We'll likely have to manage not only our feelings about the harm, but *also* those relating to the way the information is delivered. This is especially true when we're first starting out and survivors don't know that they can safely approach us and shelter with us. Before we establish a reputation for being the kind of people who keep themselves and their friends accountable, we're most likely to receive information about harm from people who are activated, which means the information will come at us in a less-than-ideal way.

....

108 The accountability auditor and educator Bianca Laureano recommended this book to me.
109 Cristien Storm, *Living in Liberation: Boundary-Setting, Self-Care and Social Change* (Seattle, WA: Feral Book Press, 2010).

Someone coming to you could be activated for many reasons. They could be the person that your friend hurt or a good friend of the person who was hurt. They could be a community member who's activated by the knowledge that harm is happening. They could be scared about approaching you because you're a friend of the person who harmed. You don't know what's going on for them, but you want a safer community, so you're going to do your best to manage your own activation so you can learn what's going on. The pause is important because it's possible that your body will react to their activation like you're being attacked. As Cristien Storm reminds us: taking a pause lets our bodies know that there is no actual danger.

Occasionally, information will be delivered by someone whose intentions don't feel right to you. For example, someone who is upset with you for another reason could suddenly divulge the information that a good friend of yours has harmed. Or someone unkind could let your friend's harm slip at the most inopportune time. The pause works here, too.

Being receptive means making a commitment to not dismiss the information simply because it was said in a way we didn't like or by someone who wasn't polite. Truth is not a stranger to unpleasantness. Someone can be activated and disrespectful, and still provide important information. Someone can be trying to upset us and our friend can have harmed. Receptivity means learning to hold various truths in our hands.

When I say that we need to offer compassion when we listen, I do not mean that we don't have a right to feel whatever feelings come up. Compassion is *not* emotional suppression. You're allowed to feel upset if someone yells at you, or if they call you a colluder and accuse you of protecting someone who harmed. Compassion does not mean that you need to be okay with any of this or pretend it's not happening. What I mean when I ask you to have compassion is to be mindful of your reaction.

Use the pause. Feel everything you feel, but react with presence and purpose. Remind yourself when your body begins to feel attacked that the other person is flailing and you have the power to stop the situation from escalating further. By not reacting aggressively yourself and remaining calm, you might prevent further escalation and may even help the other person begin to shift out of a state of activation. You could try saying, "I care about what you are telling me," or something else that affirms that you are willing to be present for what they have to say. I never stop being surprised how often it works—both with others and with me.

We *want* to be heard. We want to know that the person we've come to takes us seriously and is willing to hear what we have to say. Sometimes, situations are scary or upsetting and we mess up the delivery. You've probably had this happen yourself. It is powerful when others meet our activation with the calm we need to shift.

I see a difference between calm and stoicism. To me, calm is a state of openness that is willing to receive. Stoicism is, in a way, a rejection of the body and, as such, it cannot provide any safety cues. I view it as a form of refusal, and I think the autonomic nervous system recognizes it that way. It's hard to connect with someone who is in a state of refusal. If it's not possible for you to remain open, then calm is not possible and it is better to end the interaction for the time being.

Ending the interaction is also a good idea if the person who's speaking to you doesn't shift out of activation. If they continue yelling, and especially if you begin to feel activated and not able to prevent further escalation, I encourage you to excuse yourself. You may say something like, "I want to learn more about my friend's harm, but I'm becoming activated and can no longer have this conversation. Please excuse me." Reaching out after you have enough time to regulate yourself—perhaps over a safer medium—serves to further illustrate that you care about the situation.

GOING DEEPER

Let's say that you helped the activated person shift to a greater state of calm, or you took a break and resumed when you were both in a better place to have the conversation. Now it's time to get some more information. Here are some things you might want to know:

» When did the harm happen?
» Does the person who got hurt have support?
» Has your friend been confronted about the harm, and if so, what did they do?

» Has anyone else in your group of friends or community been told about the harm?

» Is the person telling you this information aware of any action that has been taken?

» Who else can you speak with to get more context?

By "context," I don't mean witnesses. You are neither a prosecutor nor a defense attorney. When I say "context," I mean other people who may have had similar experiences with your friend, such as people they once dated, former friends, colleagues, and so on. If this feels invasive, I want you to remember two things: The first is that the intention of this approach is not to recreate the criminal justice system and punish your friend. The intention is to take care of one another, which includes helping each other recognize harmful patterns of behavior, examining where they originate within us, and finding ways to change. To learn more about those patterns, you may need to do things that feel a little unconventional to you, such as reaching out to people you don't know very well to check in. (I'll get to how to do that in a bit.) The second thing is that doing this kind of outreach to a friend's exes, former colleagues, and friends is only considered invasive in certain subcultures. Knowing other people in a friend's life well enough to ask if they have concerns is common in many less individualist cultures, as well as small towns, islands, and some of the smaller communities that make up large cities. In the Bay Area queer community, for example, it's largely considered a red flag if someone *isn't* friends with most of their exes and willing to introduce you to them. If you don't know a new partner's exes already, you're bound to meet them—probably sooner rather than later. I think this is healthy. The isolation that occurs in communities that emphasize privacy over connection has profound implications for safety. Many of us blindly accept that value. We don't have to.

If you notice yourself becoming reactive as the conversation moves on, remember that you have the power to stop. You don't have to force yourself to push through. It's okay to ask the other person to give you a minute to take care of yourself or ask if it's okay to talk some other time. You can say something like, "This is very hard for me to hear because the person who harmed is my friend but I really appreciate you telling me what you know. I need to take a break for now to take care of myself, but I hope we can finish this conversation."

It's likely that the person you're talking with will ask you what you intend to do with the information they're giving you. It's okay to say that you don't know yet. How we decide to respond to harm depends on a lot of variables, most of which are unknown when we first learn what happened.

This is a good time to ask the person you are speaking with if they have concerns. Are they afraid of retaliation from your friend? This is important for keeping others safe, and it could also have something to offer about the shape of your friend's pattern of harm. Sometimes, the original harm is only one at the center of many others that unfold as a person refuses to take responsibility.

Another question you'll probably want to ask is whether the person you're talking to is open to answering more questions later.

TAKING TIME

Be gentle with yourself as you digest the reality that a friend has done harm. You might feel like you have do something about the situation right away, even when the harm is five years old. It's easy to confuse our own activation with a crisis-level task item. Use the pause. It's okay if it takes you a little time to process what you have learned. Remember that being willing to confront harm does not mean you have to respond immediately. If you skipped over Chapter 5, now is a good time to go back and read it.

I believe with all my heart that helping our friends take responsibility for the harms they caused will bring our communities closer and strengthen our bonds with one another. I also know that this work is hard. That's why I don't think you should do this alone. I've done it alone and it is terrible. It absolutely, positively sucks. This stuff is hard even with friends who want to own the harm they've done and want to grow and make changes in their lives. Take some time to process then get some support.

THINKING BACK

For additional context about a friend who has harmed, turn to your own memories. When we share stories, when we joke around, when we comment on the world around us, we're also sharing our beliefs. Is harm something your friend has taken lightly in the past, or joked about? When harm came up in another context, what was their response? Were they more concerned about the heartbreaking impact of harm, or privacy and reputation?

When I do these overviews, I think not only about specific harm, but others that have a similar signature. For example, in situations where people feel entitled to the time or bodies of others, you may also look for instances of entitlement to the ideas or belongings of others. In the time that I have been doing this work, I've learned that harms don't occur in isolation, a belief corroborated by the research of Leigh Honeywell and Valerie Aurora. Analyzing cases in the tech industry, Honeywell and Aurora found that people who engage in harms of entitlement "also faked expense reports, plagiarized writing, or stole credit for other people's work."[110] They call this idea of a connection among harms the Al Capone Theory of Sexual Harassment, after the American mob boss who was put away not for murder or smuggling alcohol, but for not paying his taxes—the one seemingly small crime he didn't bother to hide.

....

110   Valerie Aurora, "The Al Capone Theory of Sexual Harassment Can Help Silicon Valley Stop Hiring Horrible People," Quartz, August 2, 2017, https://qz.com/1043588/the-al-capone-theory-of-sexual-harass-ment-can-help-silicon-valley-stop-hiring-horrible-people/

"Ask around about the person who gets handsy with the receptionist, or makes sex jokes when they get drunk, and you'll often find out that they also violated the company expense policy, or exaggerated on their résumé, or took credit for a colleague's project," writes Aurora. "More than likely, they've engaged in sexual misconduct multiple times, and a little research (such as calling previous employers) will show this."[111]

I believe this is true not only about harms of entitlement, but all harms. Our beliefs and programming inform all of our actions, not only those that are potentially harmful to other humans. And while many people try to keep secret the harms they do that they can't justify, they don't do this with harms that they can. As their friends, these justifiable harms are what we see most often. Cheating is a great example. We don't shun a friend who cheats but someone with a history of cheating may well be someone who doesn't think that there's anything wrong with operating without another person's consent or denying someone's accurate perception of reality. Someone who frequently encourages people to not be boring and have another drink may well be someone who tests limits.

There are many things that we do see but normalize. I don't mean to suggest that we should look at our friends with suspicion, only that we should begin to examine our own experiences of them for traces of the beliefs and reactions that make harms possible. And we would do well to also consider how we participate in normalizing harm.

....

111   Aurora, "The Al Capone Theory."

CALLING ON OTHERS

Confronting harm is tough to do alone, so I recommend reaching out to mutual friends. Many of us are taught while growing up that talking about others is gossiping and impolite, so you may experience resistance just reading that recommendation! Your concern is valid. I don't disagree with your hesitation—talking about people can be used to turn others against them, and we know that isolation is debilitating to social mammals.[112] Also, I support any norms that encourage us to be careful with our words. I think nuance is important, though. Talk can be used to isolate, but it can also be used to bring people together and keep people safe. The context is important. We make allowances when we share good news about others, for example, or when the news is not so good and we suspect someone could use a little support. Harm is not good news, but it is a situation that requires support. We are not sharing it with the intention of ostracizing our friend, but with the desire to rally around them to help them.

On the ethical level harm is not a private matter. It does not happen in a vacuum. Harm affects not only the person who was harmed, but the people in *their* lives. Because harm ripples, and because there's a chance that it may recur, it must be seen as a breach in the peace, which changes priorities. When peace is breached, we cannot favor politeness. We must give precedence to safety. To quote Yonatan Zunger, whose powerful essay about tolerance informs my

112 Grassian, "Psychopathological effects of solitary confinement."

view on this topic: Ours "is an agreement to live in peace, not an agreement to be peaceful no matter the conduct of others."[113]

When you approach friends about the situation, make sure they understand your intention. You can put it up front and say: "I am worried about our friend. I've learned they harmed and I want to help and support them in doing accountability, and making sure harm doesn't happen again. Will you join me?" Or you can put the ask first: "I need your help in supporting our mutual friend who has accountability pending for harm. I really care about them and am concerned about this."

The Loneliest Whale

The process of checking in with other members of your friend group or community often has the unintended consequence of showing you who cares about preventing harm and who doesn't. Those who don't, or who fear having to own their harm, may respond by putting distance between you. The result is that you'll be left in the company of people who deeply care about preventing harm and transforming their communities, which is an incredible way to live. This change in your social circle has its growing pains, though—I had some lonely moments at first. I think most of us do. But this change was and remains worthwhile to me.

....

113   Yonatan Zunger, "Tolerance is not a moral precept," Extra Newsfeed, January 2, 2017, https://extranewsfeed.com/tolerance-is-not-a-moral-precept-1af7007d6376

And I've been surprised, too. Fear and self-interest caused some of my friends to disappoint me, but people aren't stagnant. We change and that change often brings growth. Sometimes it's fast—all they need is to see other people they respect stepping up. Other times, it takes a little longer—they have to see an accountability process unfold before they're ready to join in. Occasionally, it takes much longer—they have to come to terms with the harm they've done in their own lives and prepare themselves for the accounting they'll be called to do by being in your orbit.

I am reminded of the story of 52, a whale that became iconic in 2013. Though there were other whales on its migration route, this whale was dubbed "the loneliest" for its unusual 52-hertz song. The media speculated that the high frequency of 52's song was preventing other whales from understanding or communicating with it and a meme was born. But two years later, data from Scripps Institution of Oceanography in California detected multiple sources of 52-hertz song. Whalesong isn't static, you see. Pitches rise and fall across species all the time. "We see this," Scripps professor John Hildebrand told the BBC.[114] "Every season they listen to each other and synchronise their songs."

We'll sing alone at times, but not for long.

I believe in us. I don't think any of us are born being effective bystanders and agents of transformation. It's something we learn. As with trauma healing, the journey

....

114   Chris Baraniuk, "The world's loneliest whale may not be alone after all," BBC. April 15, 2015, http://www.bbc.com/earth/story/20150415-the-loneliest-whale-in-the-world

is not linear—we circle back to lessons over and over, each time learning new things about ourselves and each other.[115] It's a powerful journey, not only for those who want to own their harm and change, but for those who support them through the process.

Be gentle with yourself and with your friends when you ask them to help you confront harm. Their fear may yet be greater than their faith. They'll get there. In time, they'll learn. Thank them for listening to your concerns, remind them that you care about your mutual friend a lot, and move on.

And if they do want to participate, ask them if they have witnessed any other instances that may indicate harm.

A Bigger Picture

Harm sometimes is very specific in its pattern, happening only in certain situations, within certain relationships, or in certain power dynamics. These patterns help explain how some of us go for so long without a clue that our friend is harming.

Learning more about a pattern like this will take a little more work, but tech can be a bonus. I've also heard of enterprising friends who combed through social media posts and found multiple survivors that way. I've never personally done that, though I do think technology can be immensely valuable in this kind of work (not long ago, I assisted a

115   Gretchen L. Schmelzer, *Journey Through Trauma: A Trail Guide to the 5-Phase Cycle of Healing Repeated Trauma* (New York: Penguin Publishing Group, 2018).

friend in fleshing out his own sneaky pattern by analyzing his direct message threads!).

If you decide to reach out to strangers about the harm, I recommend not beating around the bush. A cloak-and-dagger routine can come off as shady. It's much better to say, "I heard that my friend harmed. I don't want that to be true, but if it is, I want to help them own their behavior and make changes so it doesn't happen again. I came to you because you used to hang out and you might know whether this is part of a pattern of behavior." (A variation of this wording may also be useful if there is a public callout and you want to publicly encourage your friend to take responsibility for the harm they did.) The best thing about responding early is that it reduces the likelihood that a callout will be necessary. This doesn't necessarily mean that the harm will be kept secret, however. Some accountability processes and harm-mitigation strategies may require some degree of disclosure.

BRINGING IT UP

You don't have to examine your friend's whole life before you talk to them, of course. The purpose of reaching out to others is to get a sense of what you might be dealing with, not to gather evidence for a court case. As I mentioned before, we're not trying to recreate the criminal justice system here. We want to encourage people who have harmed to own their actions, recognize their impact, and get help so they don't continue to harm.

You might prefer to let a friend who harmed know that you've heard about the harm and that you intend to talk to other people in their life about the situation. Telling them before you reach out to others gives you an opportunity to explain the purpose. I like this approach because it's open, and by virtue of being less adversarial, it increases the likelihood that my friend who harmed will join me in the process of exploration. But every situation is different, and what you decide will have as much to do with the variables you're dealing with as it does with your personal preference.

Reactions

One time, I called in a friend and something magical happened. I named the harm he had caused me, and explained how it appeared to be part of a much wider pattern.

I'll never forget his response. He said, "Oh, shit. Are you okay? I am so sorry."

Starting the conversation this way is the absolute best-case scenario. It's only happened for me once. I think I'm very lucky.

The truth is that I don't know how your friend will react. This is why it might be useful for you to recruit mutual friends early on—you don't want to make your friend feel like people are ganging up on them, but it can be helpful to have others around if you think your friend might become so reactive that they need containering.

I wish there were a good predictor of how someone will react when confronted with their harm. I've hypothesized that it requires self-esteem to look at the harm we've done and not fall apart. But how do you measure self-esteem?

I don't know how your friend will react. I don't know what your friend is like. I can only tell you to trust your gut and share how some of my friends have reacted. I've held my friends as they cried. I've had them enchant me with empty promises of change and send me right back out the door, only to have to return later on. I've had friends go into a collapse response. And I've watched friends turn different colors as they sat before me in silent rage. (That one is still a little scary to think about and I'm glad I wasn't alone at the time, even though I didn't feel I was in physical danger.)

I'm not telling you this to scare you. It's just something you should know. Confronting our harm is not easy. The first time someone told me how my actions had harmed them, I vomited.

§

I'd never tell a survivor to go gently when approaching the person who harmed them, but if you are approaching this as a friend to the person who harmed, I can tell you: Go gently. Notice your friend's reactions in their body and decide whether you need to pause to help them regulate and take care of themselves. (I discuss how activation impacts the body in Chapter 1.)

You never know how long the conversation is going to be. Occasionally, these conversations take a long time because you need to take a lot of pauses to regulate. Processing the fact that harm happened with the person who did the harm can be exhausting. This is why I don't think the people they harmed should have to take on this part of the process. It's a lot of work, and some interactions can become harmful if we don't pay attention to the distribution of power. Go with care.

Start early if you can, and do it somewhere comfortable for your friend and safe for both of you. Bring food if you aren't sure it will be readily available. Take pauses to use the bathroom and drink water. Take care of the humans in the difficult conversation. Remember that providing your friend with a feeling of safety doesn't require you to pretend that the harm didn't happen. Sometimes all it takes to calm someone down is reminding them that you still love them and that, while their actions were bad, they themselves are not.

If your friend is too activated and you can't bring them to calm, consider putting the discussion on hold until a later date. I don't recommend that you leave them while they're activated, though—if you are also activated and have no one else with you, consider calling over mutual friends to help take care of both of you.

Talking It Through

Confronting harm is difficult and you are bound to meet resistance. Here are some of the most likely forms you'll encounter:

Nah Uh!

A friend might tell you that the survivor is overreacting, or try to convince you that the harm isn't actually a harm. Your friend is someone you trust, and you may want to believe them—but sadly, we don't get to decide whether something we did harmed someone or didn't.

Honest Mistakes

Your friend might tell you it was an "honest mistake." An honest mistake is when someone harms, owns the harm and its impact on others, and takes steps to make some kind of repair. That's an honest mistake. If the phrase is being used to suggest that harm didn't actually happen because the person who harmed didn't mean to harm, that's not very honest, is it? I poured my tea onto my laptop while writing this book. I didn't mean to do it, but the laptop was still ruined. Intent and impact are different things.

When you redirect your friend's attention to the impact of their actions, listen to how they talk about the person or people they harmed. If they seem more concerned with evading responsibility than the fact someone came to harm, gently try to bring their attention back. You can cut to the chase the way the performance artist, mental health professional, and social justice activist Tas Al-Ghul taught me, by asking, "Do you care whether or not people get hurt?"

It's Justified

Sometimes people try to justify the harm they've done by implying that the person they harmed did something to deserve it. It's really hard to run into this reasoning with a friend. If they make this argument, take a breath and bring the conversation back to the impact. You can say something like, "It sounds like you're blaming the person you hurt for what happened. Let's get back to the impact."

Because ... Reasons

The other day I saw a shirt that said, "In my defense, the moon was full and I was left unsupervised." I don't think I've ever heard anyone put it quite so creatively, but that's basically what it amounts to when a friend who harmed starts to list all the factors that were in play at the moment the harm happened. It's not that our environment and situations don't affect us—it's that I think we have a responsibility to others when we cause them harm, regardless of what else we had going on at the time.

I'm not opposed to letting a friend talk about the things that were happening at the time that they harmed. Sometimes, when the harm is part of a larger pattern, these seemingly meaningless details matter. I learned this from the accountability auditor Michón Neal, who taught me that intent matters in accountability support. A survivor will naturally want the focus to be on witnessing the impact of the harm, but when we're helping someone who harmed recognize their harm, we will want to hear what they were trying to do when they harmed. Sometimes the things we intend are lovely but the methods are not. If harm is likely every time your friend tries to do a specific thing, part of the process will need to focus on re-patterning the way they do that thing.

Derailing Dismissals

"Oh, that person is just saying that because they don't like me." It might be true that the person doesn't like our friend who harmed, but does that necessarily mean that the harm being named is a lie? Why are so many of us convinced that truth-speakers are always very calm, righteous, and polite? I have learned some very important truths about myself from people who no longer like me, *especially* exes who were fed up with me and had nothing left to lose if they told me the truth.

If a friend takes this route, bring the conversation back by saying, "I'm sorry to hear that you don't have a good relationship with this person. I'm here to talk to you about the harm. Can we do that?"

Past Lives

There is nothing like that halfway point between avoidance and accountability where a friend vaguely acknowledges their harm by saying it happened—but it was a long time ago. Youthful indiscretion! They've changed now. They don't need a process. It's all good! And they don't really need to own the harm, do they? It was all *so* long ago. Everyone makes mistakes!

Yes, everyone makes mistakes! We would do well to own them and take responsibility for their impact on the lives of others.

As you talk to your friend, gently bring their attention back to the impact of their actions when they try to evade. If they become activated, help them regulate. If they start to go into a shame spiral, remind them that their actions are wrong and they themselves are not.

The best part about a call-in is that you can moderate the conversation to help your friend manage their feelings as they come up.

WRAPPING IT UP

This gentle approach can help a friend navigate much of the resistance they'll feel to owning their harm. That said, it's rare that they'll come out on the other side of accountability in a single conversation. That's okay. You came, you named the harm, you spoke to them human-to-human, and you helped them stay calm and work through some of their resistance. Now you reiterate that you want accountability for them and that you want to help them.

Your friend might ask you what accountability means. Creative Interventions has the best answer I've seen to this question. They describe accountability as a staircase consisting of six steps.[116]

1. Stop the immediate harm
2. Recognize the harm
3. Recognize the consequences of harm without excuses, even if unintended
4. Make repairs for the harm

....

116 Creative Interventions, "Creative Interventions Toolkit."

5.   Change harmful attitudes and behaviors so that violence is not repeated
6.   Become a healthy member of your community

"Rather than walking up the staircase one step at a time, one might consider the progression as more of a dance," they write. "One may be dealing with more than one step at a time and at times may move from one step to another and back again."

When There's a Callout

The more we're willing to listen to others, the sooner we'll be able to intervene with friends who are harming and the less likely a callout will be. Unfortunately, when we first start doing accountability in our circle of friends, it's much more likely that we'll be called on *because* a callout happened.

Advise your friend not to be impulsive in response to a callout. Invite them instead to have a conversation with you and other mutual friends who want to help with accountability. This is a perfect opportunity to begin forming a pod—a group of people your friend trusts and respects who can help undertake the work of keeping your friend stable and helping them along the process of accountability. (For a closer look at pods, see Chapter 3.)

It's good to have friends in an accountability pod to help the person who harmed regulate themselves. However, it's also important to include people who have enough emotional distance from the person who harmed that they'll be able to point out if the pod is sliding into collusion territory.

MANAGING THE FLAILING

Your friend will probably be defensive and upset after a callout. This is not unusual. Confronting the harm we have done isn't easy for any of us, and doing it in public can be pretty intense. It's not uncommon for people who are called out to become reactive and lash out. When the person who harmed has a lot of power or social capital, reactivity can lead to brutalizing types of retaliation. In a perfect world, tigers don't swat at house cats, but we don't live in the perfect world. The first job of a pod, then, is to create a container for the person who harmed so they can have their feelings and flail as much as they need to without harming others.

It may fall on you to remind your friend that callouts don't originate in a place of vengeance, but one of fear. A callout indicates that the people making it feel powerless to address the issue through a more direct avenue, perhaps as a result of a power differential or isolation. A callout may also indicate that they believe that your friend is a danger to the community.

Facing the impact of our actions can be really hard. It can rub against our core wounds in all kinds of ways, and dredge up any number of intensely negative feelings: shame, anxiety, unworthiness, shock, dread, horror, and even disgust. Your friend will be no different. This is one of the reasons it matters so much that they have you and other friends doing accountability support. Your commitment to your friend helps to remind them that they're not garbage—despite what they did, you and other people they care about still believe in them.

It's okay to reassure someone who harmed. The person is not the behavior. But be careful you don't say anything that sounds like you are excusing their behavior or minimizing the impact of their actions.

I learned from the relationship and intimacy coach Alex S. Morgan that it can be very difficult for the romantic partners of people who harm to be part of the latter's accountability pod. Because the process of becoming accountable can be activating to the person who harmed, their partner—who already helps them regulate on a daily basis—may become overwhelmed by the level of emotional labor that's suddenly expected of them. This creates a very strong incentive for romantic partners to enable and collude. As the process gets underway, have someone check in frequently with the partner to make sure they also have support and are taking care of themselves.

HAVING THE TALK

When things are a little calmer, ask your friend to help you understand what happened, and then listen to them with fortitude, receptivity, and compassion (see "Being Ready" earlier in this chapter). The callout introduces activating elements that are easier to avoid when friends do a call-in. For example, a callout is unlikely to avoid activating language. In fact, a callout is most likely to use this language to make sure the message is clear. If your friend becomes fixated on the language of the callout, gently bring the conversation back to the impact of their actions. You can say something like, "I hear that you disagree with the word being used. We don't have to use it. I want to talk about the fact that someone got hurt. Can we do that?"

If your friend is able to acknowledge something happened, even if they do not use the same word as the one used in the callout, ask them to sit with the impact of their actions. You can ask them if anyone else has ever expressed to them similar feelings after interacting with them. If you hear resistance or unwillingness to consider others' feelings, point this out gently. Remind them that everyone is capable of harm, and that you care about them and believe in their ability to recognize that they harmed.

ACKNOWLEDGING THE CALLOUT

I think a callout should be addressed as quickly as possible by *somebody*. It doesn't have to be the person who harmed, but a callout is disruptive and knowing it has been acknowledged by the friends of the person who harmed helps survivors stabilize and reduces community-wide activation. The more friends who respond in good faith, the better. It doesn't have to be a long message. You can say, for instance, "I am a friend of theirs and I know they'll take responsibility for the harm they have caused," or, "As a friend of the person who harmed, I am committed to helping my friend own and become accountable."

When the person who harmed is calmer, they can post their own response. They don't need to wait until they have a complete game plan for accountability to do it. It's enough for the person who harmed to issue a simple statement of intent, such as: "I've been called on to consider the impact of actions I took that deeply harmed a member of my community. I'm currently organizing a group of people to help me navigate the next steps toward accountability and repair. I don't need to be defended or affirmed at this time, and I don't approve attacks on members of the community who made the callout, or who continue to speak up about my behavior or its impact."

That's it. It can even be shorter. When I was called out on Twitter in 2018, my statement of intent was less than 140 characters long. I said simply: "I have some accounting of my own to do. Please stand by for thread. It will be pinned on my profile."[117] The full inventory of how I'd messed up took me a few days to complete and post, but that initial tweet was enough to show intention. Activation is reduced when the person who harmed shows they're listening and that they care about accountability and repair.

....

117   A.V. Flox (@avflox), Twitter, January 19, 2018, https://twitter.com/avflox/status/954504424642129920.

MAKING A PLAN

Sometimes callouts are issued along with recommendations and, other times, community members step up to make these recommendations after the callout. As a community member, you can also provide recommendations for the person who harmed to implement in their plan for accountability. Recommendations generally fall into three categories: repair, change, and harm reduction.

Repair

Not all survivors want repair, but some do, and they may issue specifications for how the person who harmed may achieve it. The most common repair task item is owning the harm. The second most common is making an apology. The third is making financial repairs, such as paying for things that were damaged or costs that a survivor incurred. A community may also make a request for repair from someone who harmed, such as by asking the person who harmed to apologize to the wider community.

Change

Task items in the change category involve suggestions about how a person may begin to examine their patterns of harm. A common request is for someone who harmed to enroll in an intervention program or a transformational course, or join some kind of support group. In the U.S., where mental health services are inaccessible to many of us, transformational coaches and alternative medicine workers are more commonly recommended than therapists.

Harm Reduction

By far the most numerous recommendations fit into the harm-reduction category. The most common of these is for someone who harmed to step down from a position of power. This request is not retaliatory. Power offers perks to a person who harmed (connections, job offers, invitations to events, etc.), and these perks can be leveraged to perpetuate silence, discourage other survivors from speaking up, and attract others who may come to harm. Requests to step down may specify an amount of time and allow for the person to return to a position once accountability has been done and some time has passed. However, if the position involves access to vulnerable members, or some other factor deemed inappropriate given the nature of the harm, a community may recommend that the person who harmed step down for good.

Another common harm-reduction recommendation is for the person who harmed to refrain from attending community events where alcohol is served, or that they abstain from drinking or using other substances at community events. A community may also recommend that someone who harmed only attend events if one or two members of their accountability pod are able to chaperone. A community may also prioritize a survivor's integration and request that the person who harmed refrain from attending certain events.

Another harm-reduction recommendation is for the person who harmed to tell prospective partners about their history of harm.

Recommendations can be valuable in giving shape to an accountability process. Though recommendations are often referred to as "lists of demands," it is possible for an accountability pod to advocate for modifications in the case of recommendations that present extreme hardship to the person who harmed.

Every once in a while, a survivor pod will be full of enterprising people who will collect accounts from all the survivors and analyze the harms and contexts, effectively doing the heavy lifting of identifying the fuller pattern of harm. If you're not so lucky, you may decide to invite other members of the accountability pod to help you continue the data-collecting you began when you first learned of the harm. Having said that, a person who harmed doesn't need to be handed their full pattern to get to work. Most people are perfectly capable of reflecting on their own life and choices—if not on their own, then with the help of a transformational coach or therapist.

Sometimes, callouts will occur without a formal request for accountability or any sort of recommendation. In that case, it is advisable for the friends of the person who harmed to proceed in forging their own path. Section 4F of the *Creative Interventions Toolkit*[118] is a fantastic place to start this undertaking.

....

118   Creative Interventions, "Creative Interventions Toolkit."

Sometimes callouts happen before a survivor gets a pod together. Sometimes communities want so much to see someone who harmed take responsibility that they rally together around them and leave a survivor unsheltered. You can use your statement of support for the process to call on the community to check in with the survivor and make sure that they are supported. (Please note: It is not advisable to use a survivor's name unless they have identified themselves.)

Measuring Success

Sometimes a friend is not ready to do the work they need to change. Sometimes they try, but the road is long and they run away and go into hiding, hoping that the situation will blow over. I've had my heart broken by a friend who bailed on the process we were helping him develop. It is a deep sorrow I hope you never have to experience.

Michelle Lisa Anderson, creator of the Love Over Addiction podcast, gave me the words to gently let friends know that our friendship would be affected if they decided to drop out of accountability. She put it like this: "I'm not willing to cross this line. This is as far as I will go. You can walk next to me, but there is a point I will need to stop. And when we reach it, I would love for you to respect me and stay with me, but if you must step over my line, you will need to do it alone. I will no longer be walking with you. I might be waiting for you if you decide to come back and join me. And I may miss you, or I may miss only parts of you. But I will not cross this line."[119]

I try not to hold my love hostage or become hostile with friends who fail to become accountable. I make clear that I care about them, but I can't hang out and pretend it's okay that they aren't willing to make the changes needed to keep others safe. If your friend drops out of their process or refuses to have one, you will have to choose what feels right to you and is most in integrity with your values.

If your friend doesn't finish their process, that doesn't mean you have failed. You did your part, and you did it well. We don't have control over what others do, only what we do ourselves. As Creative Interventions puts it: "Though resulting positive changes might not be immediate, visible, 'enough' or lasting, these efforts to intervene in violence are a big deal. They rise above silence, passivity, and inaction, and make peace and wellness in our families and communities something we work, not wait for."

Take the time you need to grieve and consider shifting your energy to supporting the members of your community affected by your friend's harm, and to increasing community resilience.

I am proud of you.

....

119 Michelle Lisa Anderson, "Episode 18: Boundary Basics – What Every Woman Needs to Know," *Love Over Addiction*, https://loveo-veraddiction.com/boundary-basics/

Conclusion

Tage Shakti Rai, who researches the intersection of violence and morality, believes it is possible to change cultures through our social relationships. "Once everyone, everywhere, truly believes that violence is wrong, it will end," he writes,[120] and I agree. But to get there, it's not enough to say we believe that harm is wrong—we have to respond when it happens. To live in alignment with this goal, we must become willing to confront harm when it happens among us. Research and experience keep showing us the power of relationships to transform. Let's use them to create the world we want.

It will not be easy to do this work. As a result of #metoo some of us are already active in standing up and joining calls for accountability. Standing in solidarity with others who are doing this work helps us prepare for confronting harm in our communities and social circles. It is among those with whom our bonds are closest that we can make the most powerful and lasting change.

We must be brave. The change begins where we are. As Jai Dulani put it in a seminal anthology about this work: "The revolution starts at home."[121]

....

120   Rai, "How Could They?"

121   Jai Dulani, "The Revolution Starts at Home: Pushing Through the Fear," *The Revolution Starts at Home: Confronting Partner Abuse in Activist Communities*, 2011, http://criticalresistance.org/wp-content/uploads/2014/05/Revolution-starts-at-home-zine.pdf

The more power or standing we have in our social circles and communities, the bigger our responsibility to confront harm in our social spheres. We are social mammals—we look to one another for direction not only about who is safe for others to be around, but what to do when we discover that someone is not. We have the power to shift one another, not just in terms of regulation but also of behavior. We can change the way things are. We can disrupt the bystanders.

If you take one thing away from this book, I hope it's this: the world we hope for is much closer than we realize. For all of our progress, the most important toolbox for this work has always been within us. We need only reconnect with ourselves and the social mammals we are.

There is a poem that technoutopians love called "All Watched Over By Machines Of Loving Grace," about a world where machines liberate humans from work and we return to the wild with other mammals to live harmoniously.[122] Just over half a century later, this seems naive, and there's some debate about whether or not Richard Brautigan was writing ironically, but it doesn't really matter. I've described the human body as a sophisticated machine throghout this book—what if all along we were the machines of loving grace?

Remember the human.

Remember *you're* human.

---

122   Richard Brautigan, *All Watched Over by Machines of Loving Grace*, 1967

Epilogue

At some point, my mother started referring to this book as my offspring, and to my process of writing it as a delivery. She didn't use the polite word one does when referring to human births, but the visceral one—the word of blood and beasts.[123] It was shocking to hear her say such a thing, and a little wounding in my more vulnerable states. But it was also brave. I think we've all gotten a little braver wrestling with this—with what it means to confront the harm among us.

This work will transform you. It's impossible to stand long before a survivor as they process what they've lived, and not get brave yourself about the experiences in your own life that have hurt you. Likewise, it's impossible to see someone recognize the harm they've done without growing the spine to confront your own. Some researchers say trauma is contagious[124] and that may be true—but then so are courage and transformation.

....

123   In South American Spanish, the verb *parir* ("to give birth") is considered vulgar. When humans give birth, the expression *dar a luz*—literally "bring to light"—is used instead.

124   Kate Coddington, "Contagious Trauma: Reframing the Spatial Mobility of Trauma Within Advocacy Work," *Emotion, Space and Society* 24 (August 2017): 66-73, https://doi.org/10.1016/j.emospa.2016.02.002

I've gotten a little braver during this long birth, this deluge of blood and screams. But I don't believe it was this book that I was birthing—it was myself. (I think of the birth of the Hecatoncheir,[125] a hundred hands groping around the birth canal at once, testing their strength on walls of warm flesh that can't and won't contain them any longer. It's a brutal image, but when are rebirths not a little brutal?)

My friend Nora Samaran asked me at some point if writing the book was healing. I said no, because I walked through each draft like Inanna[126] through one of the seven gates of the underworld, shedding more and more of the self she knew herself to be until she stood naked at the throne of death. But that's not really the whole story, just as what ends up in the book never is.

I agreed to write this book at the same time that I began to accept that I had a much more complex history with trauma than I had previously acknowledged. If I achieved what I set out to do, you won't be distracted by my journey in reading it. You'll be able to read the book in a single sitting and quickly get a sense of your rights and responsibilities—as a friend to a survivor or to a person who harmed or both—and an idea of how to get started. But, if I'm honest, it took a while to get here. Many of the

....

125   One of three giants born of Gaia in pre-Olympian Greek myth, each with a hundred hands. They later assisted in overthrowing the Titans.

126   An important ancient Sumerian goddess also worshipped by other peoples of Mesopotamia, including the Akkadians. Inanna is said to have brought civilization to humankind at Sumer after smuggling its tenets to those early people, as well as generating some of her own.

earlier drafts had nothing to do with the book I was supposed to be writing. One would become a letter to myself, full of explosive truths that I still haven't brought myself to read. Another, written in fire and bile, attempted to hold my rage—but it escaped, as Fenrir[127] always does in the end. (It would be a while before I learned how to show proper respect to my anger so it stopped breaking loose, destroying the furniture, and trying to devour the world. And it took my friend Luciano Garbati's beautiful statue *MYthology in Reverse. Medusa with Perseus' Head* for me to fully articulate the value of anger in healing.)

The book wasn't the journey, but the journey made itself manifest through it.

The journey makes itself manifest everywhere.

At each gate, I shed another aspect of myself. I shed my certainties, my beliefs, my coping strategies, my needs, my rage, my terror, and finally, myself. I surrendered. Like Inanna, I met death and was released—but not before she exacted her price, as she does. No one I know who's made this journey has slipped by Ereshkigal[128] without paying

....

127 One of the children of the Norse god Loki and the giantess Angrboða, Fenrir is a giant wolf whose size and strength so frightened the gods that they resolved to chain him for eternity. Despite all precautions, he is destined to break free and kill the god Odin during the great battle that will mark the twilight of the gods.
128 Inanna's older sister and goddess of the underworld in Sumerian and Akkadian mythology. When Inanna makes her journey to the underworld, Ereshkigal has the seven gates locked and demands that Inanna give something up to pass through each one. Ultimately, Inanna is able to leave the underworld, but Ereshkigal demands someone remain in her stead. Inanna offers up her consort Dumuzid.

their due. But she was fair to me, taking only what no longer fit into the life of the woman I had become along the way.

I don't know who you'll become as you undertake the work to confront harm in your social circle, your life, and yourself. But I know that I believe in you.

Index

Also by Thorntree Press

Ask: Building Consent Culture
Edited by Kitty Stryker, with a foreword by
Laurie Penny

"There are certain conversations that deepen
how you think; positively impact how you act;
expand your view and understanding of the
world, and forever alter how you approach
it. This book is full of them. Make room for
it—then spread the word."
— Alix Fox, journalist, sex educator and
    ambassador for the Brook sexual wellbeing
    charity

**Love's Not Color Blind: Race and
Representation in Polyamorous and
Other Alternative Communities**
Kevin A. Patterson, with a foreword by Ruby
Bougie Johnson

"Kevin does amazing work both centering the
voices of people of color and educating white
folks on privilege. His words will positively
influence polyamorous communities for years
to come."
— Rebecca Hiles, The Frisky Fairy

It's OK, Feelings, I Got You: Therapeutic Comic Drawing
Tikva Wolf

"If you are looking for a new way to manage some intense or uncomfortable emotions, communicate with partners, or for an inexpensive gift that people probably don't have but really need, I strongly encourage you to check out this awesome book! While it is good for folks in polyamorous relationships, it is not specific to relationships of any sort and is even great for kids!"
—Dr. Elisabeth Sheff

Playing Fair: A Guide to Non-Monogamy for Men Into Women
Pepper Mint

"Whether you're new to nonmonogamy and trying to chart a course or an old hand trying to find a better route to your destination, this is a brilliant road map for a more conscientious approach to ethical nonmonogamy."
—from the foreword by Kevin A. Patterson, creator of Poly Role Models and author of *Love's Not Color Blind*